Also by
Anka Radakovich

the wild girls club:

Tales from Below the Belt

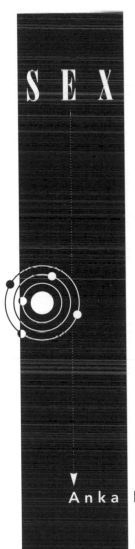

SEXplorations

journeys

to the

erogenous

frontier

Anka Radakovich

Crown Publishers, Inc.
New York

Published by Crown Publishers, Inc., 201 East 50th Street, New York, New York 10022.
Member of the Crown Publishing Group.

Random House, Inc. New York, Toronto, London, Sydney, Auckland

http://www.randomhouse.com/

CROWN is a trademark of Crown Publishers, Inc.

Printed in the United States of America

Design by Lynne Amft

Library of Congress Cataloging-in-Publication Data is available upon request.

ISBN 0-517-70195-2

10 9 8 7 6 5 4 3 2 1
First Edition

To the family unit:

Mom, Dad, and Jim Radakovich

ACKnowledgments

Love and thanks to my dauntless publisher, S. I. Newhouse, Jr.; my erogenous editor, Betty A. Prashker; my throbbing agent, Jim Stein; talented photographers Mark Abrahams, Guy Aroch, Andrew Brusso, Regina Casagrande, John Minh Nguyen, Eline Mugaas, Anna Palma, Joe Pluchino, and Jim Radakovich; and to my stimulating *Details* readers.

CONtents

sexual revolution resuscitated   9

The Naked Truth: Nature Girl Dares to Go Bare
at a Nudist Colony 13
I Do, I Do, I Do: Walking Down the Aisle of Group
Marriage 23
The Swing Set: Swinging Singles Go to a Couples-
Only Sex Club 31
Unconventional Behavior: Swinging at the
Wife-Swapping Convention 37

sexcapades

(Drag) King for a Day: My Life as a Man 45
Whip it Good: Dominatrix for a Day 55

sexcursions

Viva Las Girls: Road Tripping to Vegas 65
Anka Does Aspen: Snowboards and Snowjobs 73
Cannes Heat: Sex on the Riviera 79
Merry XXXmas: Hometown for the Holidays 87

win a date with anka

Win-a-Date I—The Contest: Stiff Competition 95
Win-a-Date II—The Dream Date: San Francisco 101
Win-a-Date III—The Sequel: New York 107

CONtents

Sextremes

Flex and the Single Girl: Getting Pumped at the
   Mr. Olympia Contest 115
Anka Anonymous: Checking into Sex Rehab 123
Looking for Mr. Religious Right: Jesus Freakin'
   Dating 131

ooohs and aaahhs

Please Come Again! Contemplating the Big O 141
Talk Flirty to Me: Hair Tossing and Winking 147
Beforeplay: First Dates 153
Anka's Secret: Lingerie Lover .159
One Night Only: Sex with a Stranger 163

Sexperiments

Wanted: Able-Bodied Men: Exciting Opportunities for
   Sexual Positions 171
Hard Science: Research Boys Get to Work in the
   Love Lab 177
Survey Says: Keeping Score 185

on-the-road testing

Babe in Toyland: I'm Playing with My Sex Toys 197
Rock Babes in Boyland: Hard-core Grrrl Talk 201
Join the (Sex) Club: I'll Take Manhattan 207

Appendix

Anka's Family Values: An Interview with Mom
   and Dad 215

SEXUAL Revolution

Anna Palma

resuscitated

the NAKED truth

Nature Girl Dares to Go Bare at a Nudist Colony

In a culture where clothes say a lot about who we are, I wondered what people would say about themselves at a place where they wore nothing at all. After "fashion week" in New York where everyone obsesses about clothes and physical perfection, I wanted to experience life in an "au naturel" setting. And what better place to shed the pretensions of the outside world than a nudist colony? It was time to strip down to the bare necessities, time to butt into the world of nude recreation.

Before I ventured out, I became a student of nudist philosophy and history, matriculating in a three-hour introductory seminar called "Dare to Go Bare," taught by the daughter of a nudist family in California whose father founded a "naturist resort." I walked out of the class with a guest pass to a nude resort and an armful of books, including *Growing Up Without*

Shame and *Beyond Nakedness*. I read all of them in the nude because, according to one book, "nudism feels good."

The cult of nudity first started in Germany at the turn of the century, presented under the auspices of medical science. Early nudists envisioned a utopian society where there would be no masks created by clothes, no barriers between each other and nature. People of all ages, shapes, and sizes would accept each other for who they were inside.

Today there is an all-nude resort town in Cap d'Agde, France, that accommodates twenty thousand nudists at a time. In America, "social nudity" was legalized in 1968 when a California state law prohibiting public nakedness was challenged. The term *nudist colony,* which implied illegality, was from then on changed to *naturist resort* or *camp,* where people enjoy "organized naturism" in a community of "like-minded people."

As I drove through the mountains of California to a "clothing optional" resort, I started to sweat. Thoughts that ran through my head included, "Will I feel self-conscious?" "Where do I look?" and "What do I do with my car keys?"

Driving up to a secluded camp nestled in the trees, I saw a sign that said FAMILY RECREATION. I continued into the parking lot. My eleven-o'clock "orientation" at the clubhouse awaited me. It wasn't a matter of *if* I would take my clothes off, but *when.* I saw a man stripping across the lot, so I decided to take it all off, starting with my Victoria's Secret thong underpants and moving up to my peek-a-boo bra. Then I sat in the car for ten minutes, wondering if my purse was large enough to cover my privates.

Finally, I opened the door and stepped out of the car. I was liberated! Free! I was walking through the gates of Eden. I was a natural woman, my pubic hair blowing in the wind.

For a minute, I thought I was having one of those dreams where I'm naked in public, except that I actually was. Then I walked up to the steps and saw seven other people—all men— waiting for the tour. They all had their clothes on. There was no turning back. I was already naked. Showing leadership qualities, I walked up to begin the tour, my seven followers trailing me, my stark-white ass bouncing up the steps. When I looked behind me and saw them hypnotized by my butt, I actually wished I'd done dingleberry check in the car's rearview mirror.

A woman conducting the tour led us around the grounds, pointing out the Zen Garden, the pool, and the Ankh Room, where they have Massage Magic Marathons (massage sessions where groups take turns on one person). As she walked us through, she told us that her daughter liked the place so much that she got married there (the priest wore only a collar).

Then she explained that "there is a special bond created when people are naked." Next, she filled us in on nudist eti- quette, noting that "looking is fine, staring is not." When some guy asked where he should look, she told him, "Directly into each other's eyes" (yeah, right). Then she told us the camp's two rules: (1) no sexual play whatsoever and no French-kissing, and (2) everyone must sit on a towel. This made sense for two reasons: You don't have to sit on a hairy bench, and it prevents caterpillars from crawling up your butt.

Since we were the first group to arrive, I sat and watched the lawn fill up with dozens of people. Soon, the tennis court was in full swing and a volleyball court was set up. (Volleyball is the number one nudist sport.) I was impressed by the different sizes of hairy and wrinkly genitalia. I became transfixed by the varying shapes of bouncing balls and bobbing breasts. The sound of flapping filled the air.

Many men have a seventies fantasy of nudist colonies as a cross between the Playboy Mansion and an outdoor sex club, with naked chicks running around and orgies every night. But in reality, the place looked more like a Diane Arbus photo of a nude Elks Club picnic. Families were picnicking on the grass, children were jumping around in the pool. It was a surreal Saturday in the park. Everything looked normal except that everyone was naked.

The fact that everyone was in the buff, that they all conformed to the same activity, gave the place a cult feel. Nudity became our camp uniform. As new arrivals walked in, those with clothes on looked like intruders.

The hundred or so nudists (about two-thirds male) included two men who looked like Ben and Jerry, a couple of Willie Nelson look-alikes, couples of all ages, a Jerry Garcia clone and his companion, a woman who looked like Bea Arthur from *Maude*. One large blanket filled up with nudie grannies, another featured two hippie women doing a body-painting thing. And one guy looked like Santa Claus with a straw hat (he had a small package).

After a couple of hours, it started to get crowded, making it impossible for me to enjoy a solitary commune with nature. To the left of me were two young guys grinning at me. To my right was a guy grinning by himself at me. As I lay on my stomach for some nude sunbathing, I was hit on with the first pickup line of the day. I heard a deep voice say, "Excuse me, Miss, I don't mean to be fresh, but do you mind if I wipe the ants off your butt?" (At least it was original.) I looked up and noticed some majorly saggy scrotum: they were dangling down to his knees. My eyes glued to his nuts, I also noticed four flies buzzing around his sack. I handed him my can of genital-strength Off!

As I sat in the Zen Garden, I found myself unable to achieve a state of relaxation. This was due to the lack of single women and the many single men eyeballing me. When I got up to go to the soda machine, I actually had the same feeling I get when I walk by a construction site. This feeling was confirmed when some guy walked up to me and said, "I really like your big nipples." "Get away from me, you creep" was my first thought, but instead, I blurted out, "Thanks, I really like your large scrotum."

Since everyone else was staring, I joined the crowd and began surveying the various configurations of pubicity and the endless grooming techniques. There were trimmed topiaries, bushy 'fros, and longhairs. (I shaped mine into a mini-mohawk.) One man who was totally shaved was sporting a rash. Another guy's shaved testicles were so shiny I could see my reflection in his balls. After fixating on people's crotches for two hours, I decided to give myself a new title: pubic affairs correspondent.

In this unclothed environment, people still distinguished themselves through accessorizing. Two men had so many piercings that their penises looked like showerheads. A sexy

and voluptuous blonde, one of the resort's resident mas-
seuses, proudly sported multiple labial piercings. One guy
used his penile piercing to amuse the other nude recreation-
ists. Through the tip of his organ was a ring that he hung his
keys on. This answered the "What do you do with your keys?"
question.

After a naked lunch, I wanted to mingle and get to know
my fellow nudists. This was no problem—people were real
friendly. As I walked around, everyone smiled at me like
Moonies. Two guys started talking to me, a thirtyish security
guard whose wife didn't join him because, he said, she's "not
into it" and a fiftyish, gray-ponytailed building contractor. I
started telling them about the nudist philosophy I had learned
at the lecture, that "nudism is honesty," that at a nudist camp
you "offer yourself, your personality." After a few minutes, I
realized that they weren't listening to a thing I was saying. I
looked down and saw two huge boners (one was bent to the
left, both were throbbing and twitching). At least at a place
like this, I could see how stimulating my conversation was.

As the three of us walked over to the soda machine, the
younger guy asked the older one if he should "put a towel on
it." "Nah," assured the ponytailed guy, "that kind of thing
happens here all the time."

Back on the lawn, I sat down with my two nature boys.
Now penilely focused, I became more and more concentrated
on a man in his seventies who had an erection the entire day
that never went down. He played tennis for an hour erect, he
walked around erect, he ate a snack erect. "What's the story
with grampa and his petrified rock over there?" I asked the

guys. "His boner is ageless," one of them told me. "Yeah, Norm got the pump," said the other one. "He has the body of a seventy-six-year-old and the boner of a seventeen year old. He just pumps it up and it stays up for days." This was truly the utopian penis. If there was another guy with one, they could have a penile pump joust.

Eventually, three more guys asked if they could bring their towels over. I now had a total of five naked guys sitting around me, campfire style. As the six of us "got to know each other," I looked at the crowd and noticed wood between their legs. It looked like Bat Day at Yankee Stadium.

To complete our trip to Shangri-la, to Walden Pond, we six naturists stepped further into paradise by enjoying the mountain views. Above the bubbling hot tub was a sign that said LEAVE YOUR HANG-UPS HERE. As I walked into the Jacuzzi with six naked guys, we were joined by a man who looked like Rodney Dangerfield. His opening line as he stepped into the Jacuzzi was "I've got a groin injury." He immediately attached himself to me and told me his life story: he has been a member of the nudist resort since '68, he never made it as an actor in Hollywood because he never got any parts, he loves to go to swingers' clubs because they really turn him on, he's a total voyeur and exhibitionist who likes to be naked, see people naked, and have other people see him naked. The whole time he was telling me this he was pulling on his "groin injury."

Also in the tub was a fifty-year-old member since '79, an ex–porno actor from the eighties who told me he shows up on the weekends to see families with young teenage daughters because they "make me hard." He also reminisced about

"penetrating a woman in the pool while a five-year-old paddled by but didn't notice."

Next to him was the ponytailed guy, an ex-playboy who
had been a member since '70. "This place really swung in the
seventies," he told me. "But it's not like that anymore. The
women who run the place really discourage sexual activity.
There are a lot of families here. Now if I want to fool around,
I have to do it in the bushes."

My fellow nudists seemed excited by our naturist talk; I
looked into the Jacuzzi and saw six underwater torpedoes
ready to launch. By this time, the boner thing was starting to
seem like a secret handshake indigenous to nudist cults. Surrounded by six nude men in a hot tub who were interested in
me but I wasn't interested in them, I felt as if I were about to
be boiled and eaten at that night's "potluck tribal dinner."

When the married guy said, "Come on, show us your
lips," I knew it was time to leave. As I moved away from him,
one of the other guys asked me if I wanted a massage. (By the
end of the day, I had over ten offers for massages.)

Would I have felt differently if the guys had all been cute?
Yep, then it would have been erotic. Then I would have been
at the Playgirl Mansion in nudie bootie utopia.

On the other hand, what I liked about the place was that
the people were not judging each other on their physical
imperfections, surprising considering the place is so close to
L.A. One of the resort's credos is about body acceptance, feeling good about your body with no shame. But as I left, I was
receiving way too much body acceptance. The married guy
asked me why I was leaving so soon, the ex-playboy guy chased

me into the parking lot, pointing to his watch and the bushes. The Rodney Dangerfield guy was saying, "Come on, just give me one more hug and I'll leave you alone!" As I jumped into the front seat to make my escape, the three surrounded my car. It was *Night of the Living Dead*. I peeled out. Although the rest of the "naturists" thought they had found utopia, I found man in his most primitive state. It was a brave nude world.

i do, I DO, i do

Walking Down the Aisle of Group Marriage

It was while sitting in that hot tub at the nudist colony that I had my first exposure to the world of group marriage. After asking one of my eight tub buds, "What's up with the single's mingle tonight?" he said, "That's for senior citizens. *You'd* really be a hit at the group marriage seminar." At least it sounded kinkier than the Overeaters Anonymous night.

At his suggestion, I was off to find a husband (or two). Since plural marriages have existed for centuries and still do (the king of Morocco supposedly had two hundred wives), I wanted to join the crowd. I wanted to live the alternative lifestyle, like Mormon polygamists in Utah or Pygmy tribes in Africa. I envisioned my harem of boys in the Middle East filled with blondes, brunettes, and redheads, until I found out that

Muslim law allows men to have up to four wives and unlimited concubines, but polyandry (a woman married to two men or more) is illegal.

According to my "polyfidelity" handbook, obscure groups of people do exist who "live the dream" of having multiple spouses. This crowd call themselves "polyamorists," who practice "polyintimacy." Poly people are into sex *and* love and deep commitment—to a bunch of people. Their philosophy is "the more the merrier" and they believe that we are capable of loving more than one person at a time—a utopian view shared in sixties hippie communes. In other words, love the ones you're with.

The poly people think that "monogamy is monotony" and believe in what they call "responsible nonmonogamy." Their theory is that multiple partners relieve sexual boredom and loneliness while offering variety and excitement. Into sharing and caring, they differentiate themselves from the swinger/wife swappers who are in it just for sex without emotional involvement. The two groups, however, could have the same bumper sticker on their Chevy minivans: TAKE MY WIFE PLEASE! . . . AND I'LL TAKE YOURS!

Polys refer to their relationships with terms such as *open marriage, group marriage, tribe, cellular family, expanded family, triad, intimate network,* or *multilateral marriage.*

Arrangements vary. Two legally married or unmarried couples, for instance, could have an "open group marriage" where they are open to outside relationships. Or they may promise sexual fidelity to the group, "polyfidelity." Or maybe an "intimate network" is created by two couples who swap with each other but are joined by Mary, an old "friend" who moved back into town who is bisexual and wants to get it on with one of the wives and two of the husbands. ("I take thee to be my lawfully wedded husband and husband and wife.")

What Ron L. Hubbard is to dianetics, Robert Heinlein and Robert Rimmer are to the utopian group-marriage devotees. Heinlein's novel *Stranger in a Strange Land* tells the story of Valentine, a human from Mars raised by Martians who travels to Earth and becomes the leader of a commune where men in their forties are married to chicks in their twenties with "firm buttocks" and Ph.D.'s in astrophysics. (They don't call it science fiction for nothing.)

Rimmer's *Harrad Experiment* takes place at a college (the title comes from Harvard/Radcliffe) where students are thrown together in a group living experiment. Both books reveal the characteristics of polys (high-IQ's, idealism, and evolved spirituality), their aspirations (total honesty and personal growth), and hobbies (tantric sex and organized nudism).

Mitch Slomiak spent eleven years on the Kerista commune in San Francisco. In one of his writings, "Coping with Jealousy on the Poly Frontier," he reported that the commune operated on the theory that jealousy would be replaced by a new emotion that they termed *compersion:* "the happiness that was felt upon noticing two or more partners having fun with other partners." To Kerista, "jealousy polluted the purity of the lifestyle laboratory." But if communal group marriages work, then why do very few exist? My theory is that either jealousy is hard to overcome, or all the women in the commune got PMS at the same time and it turned into a bitchfest.

Since the San Francisco Bay area has the reputation as sex radicalism headquarters, it was there I went in search of the "poly people." I signed up for a "new paradigm relating group" in Marin County that my resident friend Lucille said was filled with "New Age guys who are into self-help."

The group met in a house in the suburbs, in what looked like an extra bedroom with no furniture and five people sitting cross-legged on cushions. Deborah, the facilitator, asked me as I entered the room to take my shoes off because it was a "sacred space."

My group consisted of Deborah, a sort of "group marriage counselor" with a Ph.D. in psychology who would lead us; Raj, a midforties Indian guy who described himself as "clothing impaired" (a nudist) who has a Swedish girlfriend he would like to share the poly lifestyle with; Doug, a fiftyish single guy who has been married a few times, can't be monogamous, wants multi-relationships, yet wants no responsibility; Shirley, a fortysomething woman who works in bio systems and wants to meet other poly people; Bob, a "Marin County guy" who is in a relationship with three women; and Sabaat, a former member of the Rajneesh cult in Oregon. Needless to say, what a group.

After the introductions, it was time for the "eye-gazing" exercises. These were designed to build the trust and intimacy needed in multipartner relationships. As I sat across from the Rajneesh guy, we were directed to stare into each other's left eye. "Breathe in, breathe out!" directed Deborah. "Open up!" she urged, flailing her arms as we held the gaze.

Hyperventilating and ready to pass out, I felt I was in a sweat lodge. But since the exercise was about caring and sharing, I transcended my discomfort and shared my sexual energy; I licked my lips and gave him a "Hello, sailor" look. As we gazed, I realized how little people in daily life look each other in the eye. I also noticed a "new member" of the group popping up in his sweatpants.

After we each switched partners, we were asked to share—with total honesty—our thoughts, positive or negative, while we were gazing. Then we were supposed to hug each other. Bob, the Marin County guy, said that as a "middle-class WASP" he was turned off by the Indian guy's "foreignness." Doug, who was looking for two women, said he felt feelings of homophobia while gazing with Bob. Then they hugged each other and felt even more homophobic.

The Rajneesh guy said that as he was gazing at me, my face kept changing. He said I turned into fifty different women, and at one point, I became a blonde. I wondered if he got laid a lot in the cult.

Once everyone opened up, they started spilling the beans. Bob confessed that he never got chicks when he was in his twenties or thirties, but now that he was forty-nine, he had to beat them off with a stick. Although he was currently involved with three women, he said tearfully that he felt humiliated for being impotent. (My analysis: a psychosomatic case of poly penile performance anxiety.)

This was my first therapy session, let alone group therapy session, let alone group-marriage therapy session. I had to make up a story on the spot or I would have seemed suspicious. I told them I was living in a triad with Gary and Lucille, a married couple, and that we were having problems with intense jealousy. Going overboard with the scenario, I pretended to be a mess. The scary part was that everyone believed me. When I added that I thought bringing in another guy would even things out, several of the guys in the group volunteered to join my extended dysfunctional family.

After the meeting, we did "group hug" and promised to meet next week. (Yeah, sure.) The next night I went to a "poly discussion group" for people in their twenties and thirties whom I'd met over the Internet to see if they were interested in this alternative lifestyle. On the way over, I brushed up on my poly pickup lines. ("Do you five come here often?")

My new "tribe" consisted of Cari, a twenty-four-year-old housewife whose interests include vampires, witchcraft, and hiking; her thirty-two-year-old husband, who enjoys UFOs and Rainbow Gatherings; Susan, a twenty-two-year-old student who grew up on a commune; her twenty-five-year-old boyfriend, who was looking for a bi-curious man to complete the group; and my future husband, a cute thirty-three-year-old hacker whose favorite hobby was hypnotism. ("You are all getting horny.") Though their attitude was more swinger-like, they still wanted to wake up the morning after a hot Roman orgy and say, "I love each and every one of you."

In theory, it seems like a possibility. I could see having a group marriage with two of my best female friends and three hunks of boy meat with brains and bulge.

I see the future now. Star date 2001. The six of us are all married and living on Planet Polywood. It's like the *Real World* except we all swap sex partners and nobody gets jealous, sexually bored, or on each other's nerves. Plus we're all naked. And we live happily ever after.

tHe SWING ʃet

Swinging Singles Go to a Couples-Only Sex Club

Put four single, jaded New Yorkers together and it becomes increasingly difficult to find cheap thrills on a Saturday night. "Let's drop the boys off at one of those places where they can get prostate massages, and we'll go to Chippendales," suggested my friend Kate.

"Let's go to the Vault," offered Ken. "I need my scrotum stretched."

"I have a better idea," said David. "Let's check out a swingers' club."

"I've heard of a place uptown," said Dawn, pulling out a suddenly handy copy of *America's Horniest People,* a swingers' magazine. "We don't have to have sex. We'll just go for a walk-through." The next thing I know we were in a cab on a quest for the free love we missed in the seventies.

As we paid the $90-per-couple entrance fee to Le Trapèze, "New York's only on-premises swing club," we were handed two temporary membership cards. Printed on the back of a drawing of a nude woman on a swing were the words "No prostitution. No cameras or recording devices. Membership is subject to approval and review." We paid our initiation fee and were ready to become bona fide swingers.

Richie, a bearded Bob Vila look-alike *(This Old Swing House)* wearing khakis and a manager tag, offered to give us an "orientation." As we began our tour, he stressed repeatedly, "You arrive as a couple and you move from room to room as a couple. There is no roaming around as a single." He asked our names and David introduced us with phony ones. I was now "Susie." Richie led us to the lounge where he said, "Relax, have a drink, but serve yourself because it's a 'private party.' Look," he added, "many people are lounging already." The decor strived to be a Bavarian inn but was more like the set for *Ski Lodge II: The Trailer Court*. Vintage girly paintings on black velvet added a great touch, and a couple of BarcaLoungers created a New Jersey tract-house feel. The patrons welcomed us with curiosity and approving eye contact, like the first couple we saw—she in big white panties and a bustier that didn't fit right and he in white Jockey briefs with stomach overhang. It looked like a playpen for naught-but-nice accountants you might see at the mall, except everyone was in their underwear.

"Everyone is nervous at first, but you'll get over it," Richie told us when he saw us giggling, then he pointed out, "At this club, we cater to the ladies."

Meanwhile, over at the pool, hunky masseurs were catering

to the ladies, loosening them up with free massages while their husbands watched. Richie then led us to the locker room, where he introduced us to Frank, the guy handing out towels, who he noted was a "famous porn star in the seventies" ("the club pro").

After our tour was over, it was time to start swinging. In the locker room, we all stripped and donned towels. Our first stop was the "mat room," a dimly lit room filled with half-naked and naked people sprawled out on fluffy wrestling-like mats. As we walked into the room, fifteen couples were fornicating exuberantly. Side by side, pairs of anonymous buttocks pumped away. I saw missionary, woman-on-top, scissors, doggy, froggie, and other advanced, pretzel-like positions. The fact that thirty total strangers were engaging in the most private acts in semipublic took us into orgy central. Adding to the group sex effect was that distinctive orgy scent ("Musk de Tuna"). The communal philosophy here was "Everybody likes it, it's no big deal, so let's all like it together."

People were clearly taking their swinging seriously. No one was laughing and most couples were too busy to speak. I did, however, hear several "Oh, baby"s, two "Don't stop"s, and one loud "Oh, Jesus!" This gave me an irresistible urge to cheer on the copulators with shouts of "Go, girl!" "Do it to her one more time!" and "Whoomp, there it is!"

The cacophony of moans, groans, and grunts was so intense that I got a c.b. (chick boner). Every five minutes, the sound of someone's orgasm went off like a snooze alarm. I closed my eyes and listened to small ones, medium ones, large ones, multiple ones, premature ones, and simultaneous ones. It was some of the best sex I've ever heard.

The only furnishings in the room were buckets of condoms and signs that said ACCORDING TO NEW YORK HEALTH CODE 52-C, FELLATIO AND ANAL SEX ARE PROHIBITED, which I wrote down. I also jotted down a new idea for a sign: DON'T TOUCH THE HEMORRHOID.

At that moment, the manager grabbed me by the arm and pulled me out of the room. We were being watched. (Being watched and watching were the essence of this place.) "A cop and his wife saw you writing and he got paranoid. He thinks you're a cop or a reporter," he said. I suppose we were a bit obvious; giggling and pointing is one thing, but giggling, pointing, *and* taking notes at a place like this would make anyone nervous. I told him I was an erotic poet. Apparently he believed me because he asked if he could read some of my work sometime. He also told me I was breaking the rules by wearing shoes. And of course, as soon as I took the shoes off, I stepped into a wet spot. I prayed that it was someone's spilled drink.

After watching a few multiple orgasms, we headed upstairs. Climbing a flight of spiral stairs gave everyone an opportunity for a little group grope. One superfriendly patron stuck his finger up my towel and touched my snoopy.

We ventured into the "semiprivate" room for "disrobed couples only," which consisted of a row of doorless cubicles, each large enough for one or two couples. The emphasis of this floor was on group voyeurism: as people licked and sucked inside the small rooms, other couples stood outside watching. As David and I checked out one couple doing "cowgirl" (woman sitting backward on top of guy), they checked us out, flirting as they pumped.

"Let's swing with them!" David suggested.

"I don't know," I said. "The Asian girl is cute for you, but her boyfriend looks like a total dork, sort of like Don Knotts in *Three's Company*."

Meanwhile, I overheard one husband and wife from New Jersey picking up another husband and wife from Brooklyn ("married but swingle"). In a place like this, pickup lines like "Do you two come here often?" make perfect sense.

Unlike a topless bar, this joint stressed equality. The "love seat" was a case in point. The chair, whose only function was to elevate a woman so she could comfortably enjoy cunnilingus, looked like a cross between a dentist's chair and the inner-thigh machine at the gym. ("We cater to the ladies.") These pleasure chairs seemed to inspire a mass munching, because all the women in the vicinity had their legs up in the air and a head in between. (As one guy came up for air, he winked at me.) I haven't seen such voracious eating since I went to the $5.95 all-you-can-eat at the Sizzler.

This oral activity seemed to arouse my three formerly platonic buds, who had moved from being voyeurs to the life of the party. In another cubicle, the triad was deep into a three-some. Did I miss something? Like flies on a fresh loaf, there was a sudden pileup of ten people watching at the door. It was as if someone grabbed a megaphone and announced, "Hey, everybody, over here! It's a three-way!" One guy stood masturbating under his towel. Another couple watched while they fingered each other's butt. Seeing my friends in a licking-stroking session made me feel left out. On the other hand, I was happy not to be ogled by strangers with beer bellies fondling themselves—I get enough of that on the New York City subway.

Once my friends were done, we all returned to the lounge, which was packed with twenty-five postorgasmic couples sharing their afterglow with others. It looked like a hospital recovery room. One couple was so worn-out, they fell asleep sitting up, their heads on each other's shoulder. (Group sex is exhausting.) Other satisfied customers were huddled in their underpants at the hot-'n'-cold buffet. One guy was holding a greasy drumstick with one hand and picking pubic hairs from his teeth with the other.

Two weeks later, I saw a news report that the health department was banning vaginal intercourse in New York City sex clubs. It must be discouraging for the most serious swingers, who will now be restricted to bush munching, and for the club's management, who will have to order more love seats to keep the crowds coming. From now on, their new slogan will be "Eat at Le Trapèze."

UNCONVENTIONAL
BEHAVIOR

Swinging at the Wife-
Swapping Convention

Once I had become a new member of the swinging scene, I put my name on the official swingers mailing list. Naturally, I was excited when I received my "exclusive" invitation to the 21st Annual Lifestyles Convention: "Join us for three days and three nights of liberation and enchantment. Simply let your hair down and enjoy an adult three days at the largest lifestyle couples gathering in the world," it said, sounding like the Super Bowl of swinging. I called my playguy and we were off to San Diego to experience the "playcouple philosophy."

As soon as we checked into our hotel, we were heavily cruised. Every flirtatious couple we saw was holding hands and smiling, looking at us as if we were fresh meat. Everyone was real friendly.

Arriving just in time for the Black and White Dance, we

put on our name tags ("Sid" and "Nancy") and ventured into the ballroom. I wore a bra, fishnets, and a black cat mask. Sid wore motorcycle boots and a black flasher raincoat that fit in perfectly with the rest of the outfits: garter belts and bustiers, togas, and towels. Couples were in their twenties, thirties, forties, and fifties—holdouts from the sexual revolution who looked as if they had been swinging since the sixties. The real action was taking place at poolside, where a literal "swap meet" was in progress. Within minutes, one of the many on-the-make couples asked if we were married; most of the nearly one thousand couples already were. One computer-programming couple told us, "We have kids and everything!" (At last year's convention in Las Vegas, one of the couples had a wedding. At the end of the ceremony, the priest said, "You may all kiss the bride.")

To get in the "lifestyle" mood, we swingled, chatting with a few couples who asked us what room we were in. Everyone looked as if they were having fun. They were shiny, happy, horny people. We speculated that their happiness was due to the fact that by the second night, they were on their third couple.

As we sat down, several couples tried to hit on us. The pickup technique went like this: a couple sat on a chair next to us, started making out, then checked to see if we were interested. Voyeurism and exhibitionism were encouraged. The woman next to us asked us, "How long have you been in the lifestyle?" then started fellating her partner. Another couple waved us over while they did doggie on a lawn chair. Another couple filled us in on the history of swinging. "Closed swing-

Andrew Brusso

ing," they told us, is when couples swap partners and then each couple goes off privately together. "Open swinging" means swinging openly, as in a foursome, in the same room, in the same bed. "What do you call that?" asked Sid, pointing to poolside, where a five-way boy-girl-boy-girl-girl oral sex thing was going on. "That's called a daisy chain," the wife told us. As we watched group 69, another woman walked by and asked, "Why don't you two join us in the Jacuzzi?" We considered it until we looked up and saw thirty couch potatoes boiling in the hot tub.

Walking back to our hotel room, we overheard people in the

next room going at it, having orgasm after orgasm. A few minutes later, eight people piled out of the room with camcorders.

Four hours later, as we awoke to more sounds of ecstasy, we didn't know whether to tell them to shut up or join them. The next day, suffering from sleepus interruptus, we went to the Sensual and Erotic Art Exhibition at what we called the Swingers' Convention Center and they called the Lifestyles Exhibit Hall. One booth offered "adult products" featuring the "realistic silicone vagina." The man behind the table informed us that "each pubic hair was individually hand-sewn." He also pointed out that the vagina was created from a mold of a porno star who would be at the masquerade ball that evening. Sid stuck his finger in it and concluded, "Wow! She's really tight!" I suggested he wash his finger because you never know where that thing had been.

Next to this booth was a guy displaying his "erotic etchings," another guy selling "access pants" for easy entry, and a third demonstrating the "love swing." One booth promoted the "love table" (described as "the best fuckin' table ever!"). As we browsed, a deadhead-looking dude insisted on rubbing lotion on my hand with the "love mitt." I made the mistake of saying, "The love mitt, the love swing, it's a whole rub, swing love thing going on here," which gave him the go-ahead to rub his schwanz against my leg.

One booth featured information on "The Edgewater West—California's premier resort hotel." According to the owner, "satisfied guests" meet in a "clothing-optional, romantic playground." Explaining the swinger's hotel etiquette, he said, "If you leave the curtains open, you want to be watched.

If you leave the door open, you want to be joined." This hotel echoed the utopian philosophy that the original swingers (or "wife swappers") believed in: nobody gets jealous; you can be in love with your spouse and have sex with lots of other people for the rest of your married life and your wife likes it (and watches).

In practice, however, jealousy happens. At one point I felt excluded when Sid got turned on by a woman whose partner was a turnoff to me. Then Sid got jealous when a porn-star guy wanted to swing with me. (The convention provided a "safe room" with a "care team" to deal with these issues.) I wanted to go to the room just to see people OD'ing on jealousy while their partners were back at the Jacuzzi getting into a threesome.

At the Exhibit Hall, one guy said to us, "Hey, you two, there's a squirtin' seminar in five minutes!" (Topic: female ejaculation.) Another seminar was entitled "Swinging Christians: Not a Biblical conflict," taught by people with Ph.D.'s in sexology from schools I'd never heard of.

After our adult education, we dressed for the grand finale of the weekend: the Erotic Masquerade Ball. I wore seventies disco while Sid went shirtless and donned the penis tie he had bought at the Exhibit Hall. One couple dressed as a topless cheerleader and a football player in a jockstrap. Other costumes included harem girls, Cleopatras, dominatrices, an angel with a devil, a Little Bo Peep, and a bunch of naughty nurses. As the conventioneers filled the dance floor, pileups occurred; one couple did the bump with another and so on until their group became a dirty dozen.

And, after the ball . . . more balling. Walking into Room 200 was like entering a swingers' orgy den circa 1972. In the darkly lit honeymoon suite, couples were groaning and groping on the couch, on the floor, and against the wall. A daisy chain was flowering on one of the beds. On another orgy bed, the ten fattest people at the convention were pumping away. A couple of the couples had the most gigantic bare butts I've ever seen. For a minute I thought I was in front of the hippo cage at the San Diego Zoo.

In the middle of it all sat a woman on a vibrating vaulting horse with a snap-on tool riding it like the bucking bronco at Gilley's. On each side of her were two men "assisting" her, shouting, "Let it go, baby!" as they held her down. As she came to a screeching halt, everyone applauded. When she stood up, she could barely walk, let alone take a bow.

On the balcony, we got turned on watching an attractive couple bent over the railing. Still, it felt like the ruins of the sexual revolution, a post-AIDS remnant of sexual liberation, a fragment of the utopian order. Or maybe we were just watching an institutionalized form of cheating on your spouse.

After a hard night of voyeurism, we went back to our room. Because trophies had been given out that evening (Sexiest Costume) I gave Sid the Sexiest Swinger award, while he crowned me Miss Orgymeister. And since everyone wanted to play with us, we proclaimed ourselves Most Popular Play Couple.

SEXCAPADES

Jim Radakovich

(Drag) King

f o r a d a Y

My Life as a Man

It's a man's world and I've always wanted to penetrate it. Since I love men so much, I fantasized about becoming one— just for a day or two. I wanted to be in a *Twilight Zone* episode where Anka turns into Harry Peters and no one notices. By switching sexual identities, I could see the world through the male gaze. I could deconstruct gender differences. I could pee on the street.

So I became a man. Well, sort of. I enlisted the assistance of a cross-dressing performance artist and member of the F2M (female-to-male) fraternity, who holds workshops to teach women how to "try on the male guise and enter the male domain." Diane's job, along with her special-effects makeup artist, John, was to metamorphose my friend Susan, myself, and three other girls into virile, studly he-men.

At first, I told John I wanted to look like a fly downtown guy. I took my lipstick off and smashed my hair down and for a minute looked like Trent Reznor. But he told me my hair was too feminine to be worn down, so he hid it under a hat. Then he went to work gluing hair onto my eyebrows and rubbing black powder on my face, making it look as if I had dark circles, blackheads, huge pores, and a five-o'clock shadow. With more makeup he simulated a cleft chin and gave me a prosthetic Adam's apple. Then he glued on a black mustache. "You will be surprised at the man you will become," Diane told us. Horrified was more like it. I took one glimpse in the mirror and realized I looked like a recent parolee (serial rapist) who just got a job as a janitor. I was no dreamboat. Susan and I had hoped to become strapping, studly, hot-lookin' guys. Instead, we ended up looking like two short, creepy, ugly sleazeballs.

After the shock of seeing ourselves as men wore off, we all sat on the floor and made fake penises out of tubular bandages and cotton balls for that Marlboro Man bulge. "Don't make them too big," Diane warned as Susan and I began constructing thick ten-inchers. "I want to be a skinny guy with a huge dick," said Susan with anticipation, stuffing her Jockey briefs with the finished product. When we were done, we were hung like a couple of Clydesdales.

Next we flattened our boobies by wrapping them with Ace bandages. After our surface identities were altered, we all learned how to sit (legs spread apart), walk (as if we owned the place), speak (with deep voices), and eat (less delicate, more caveman). We practiced on beer nuts and beef jerky. I showed the girls how to burp. John told us how to pee (men don't wipe, they shake it dry).

Next, we were told to develop a character based on our new appearances. If clothes make the man, then my plaid shirt, black jeans, and big black boots made me Jose, a drug rehabilitation counselor from the Bronx. My friend Susan turned into Lee, a gay club kid who likes to dance and do ecstasy. Diane became a retail manager at Macy's, two other girls couldn't figure out who they were, and another girl, an editor at *Ms.* magazine, became Steve, who said he worked at *Details* as the editor of the sex column.

After two hours in the workshop, we hit the outside world. Feeling like actors without a script, we got stage fright. Walking out of the loft, we wondered if our masquerade would be detected. Would we pass as men or would we just look like a bunch of trick-or-treaters?

To test our new identities, we took cabs to a restaurant. "Lee" and I took our own cab so we could make fun of each other's stupid mustaches. For a minute, we felt like Lucy and Ethel. Two minutes into our foray as "men," the cabdriver asked, "Do you mind if I ask you two a question?"

"Go ahead, ask what you want," I said in my manly voice.

The driver, who was wearing a turban, asked, "Are you two guys heterosexual or homosexual?"

I said, "Homosexual," at the same time Lee said, "Heterosexual."

Then the driver asked, "What does the sperm taste like?"

"It's salty," I told him.

"It can be cheesy," added Lee.

"So what is it, salty or cheesy?" the driver wanted to know.

"It kind of tastes like chicken noodle soup," explained Lee. Finally, we both agreed that it tasted like French onion soup with boogers.

After that, the driver had to know, "When you stick the dick up there, where does the shit go?"

At the restaurant, we felt like gender impostors, Bond girls working undercover. We ordered with our new deep voices and went undetected. Ignored was more like it. The cute waitress neglected all of us at the table except for the desirable *"Details* editor."

The fact that we were passing gave us confidence to visit a place most women rarely patronize, the local strip bar. As we walked into the all-nude club, we joined thirty other men who were watching Berlin-style cabaret acts, including the dancing nude stripper with Mardi Gras mask, and the naked fire-eating chick. A third woman's routine consisted of spreading her legs on a chair for a roomful of strange men, who only tipped her $10. After showing her slice, she got only enough money for a large pie.

This is when one of the strippers came over to our table and asked if anyone wanted a lap dance. "I'll have one," I said, real macho as she led me over to the "adultery couches." When she started gyrating her hips, peeling off her bra, and pushing her knockers in my face, I picked the worst possible moment to develop a case of the giggles. Thoughts that entered my mind during the lap dance included "There are eight real guys sitting at the bar watching who are too cheap to buy a lap dance," "Get off me, I'm a gay man," and "Your nip-

ple rings are scraping off the glue on my fake eyebrows."
Needless to say, I remained completely flaccid.

First she felt the Ace bandages on my chest and said,
"Nice pecs."

"Yeah," I said, "I've been working out."

Then she put her hand on my prosthetic penis and said real
deadpan, "Wow, you're really packin'!"

"It's pretty big," I bragged, "but it's a little lumpy."

Freud once said, "When you meet a human being, the
first distinction you make is, male or female?" and you are
accustomed to making the distinction with unhesitating cer-
tainty. Freud should have checked out our next stop: Sally's
Hideaway II, a transvestite pickup bar where we went to see
how drag queens would react to us drag kings. I figured that
if anyone would see through my guise it would be a fellow
cross-dresser. But apparently not. As we watched the "topless
she-male dancers" circling the bar with their pimps, one
"pretty woman" who looked like a bad Eartha Kitt sashayed
by, tweaked my drawn-in cleft chin, and growled, "Hey,
tiger!" One she-he had shaved his chest and put concealer on
his nubs, an attempt to hide the five-o'clock shadow on his
breast implants. When "she" hit on me, I wondered what it
would be like having a trick with one of the chicks with dicks.
I figured that if a woman cross-dressed as a man had sex with
a man cross-dressed as a woman, then we would be having
straight sex.

Even going to the bathroom was confusing: both the
men's and ladies' rooms were filled with men in dresses. The

suffocating smell of ammonia in the men's room left me with no other choice but to use the "ladies'" room. As I walked in, a bunch of guys dressed as women wouldn't let me in because they thought I was a guy. In reality, I was the only real woman in the whole place. I passed as a john, yet I couldn't find one to use. My bladder had become gender-bent out of shape.

The next day, I continued my adventures in manliness, but this time I became "Luc" and asked John to make me look like a hot guy in a cool band. I was still short, but I wanted to be less ugly. John attempted to lighten my hair, to make me look like a blond, but my spray-on hair went haywire and I ended up with gray hair. I took one look at the "special effects" makeup in the mirror and saw an unattractive loser in his late forties with a gray ponytail who had seen too many Grateful Dead concerts.

Nevertheless, my gay friend Rick and I were now ready for our boys' night out. Our first stop was an all-male peep show, where I had my first exposure with "buddy booths." These consisted of a row of telephonelike booths equipped with a video screen for male porn and "glory holes," rectangular slots on each side of the wall, waiting for the insertion of the male "pal." When I crouched down for a peep, I was greeted by a pair of willing lips. I guess this was what a "buddy" was all about.

Women could never have sex like this. We want to at least see the other person's face first. I can't imagine girls sticking their genitalia into a hole in the wall, then letting someone (anyone) suck them in a "Betty booth."

Next it was off to a gay male sex club for some man-to-man bonding. As we paid $20 admission, my heart was pumping out of my chest. I was terrified of getting caught, yet at the same time it was exciting. First we walked into a movie theater where we checked out the latest in all-male porno films. I give *Jock Strapped* two thumbs up for its all-male dialogue ("Give it to me, you big prick"). Then we went downstairs to a dimly lit, low-ceilinged room where some heavy cruising was going down. As we walked through a hallway of cubicles, nobody suspected that I was anything other than a man. In fact, I was very popular. I felt like the "It" boy. One guy stood in a cubicle ushering me in with his eyes. (Rick told me that meant he wanted to "receive.") A second guy sat in a cubicle. (That meant he wanted to "give.") Another guy looked me in the eye as if he wanted me bad, then rubbed his crotch. I cruised him back and grabbed my phony baloney. This is when Rick cruised by and whispered in my ear that I was doing it wrong: I should grab it more to the left.

No one spoke. It was completely physical. As Rick and I sat in one of the larger cubicles, I asked him, "How fast does it happen?" "Real fast," he told me. Two minutes later, one of the guys who was cruising me walked into the room, shut the door, and unzipped his pants, not saying a word. I heard no sounds of seduction, but I did hear sounds of suction. Suddenly, I was having three-way sex with two gay men. Okay, so I was just watching. Five minutes later, it was over. As he zipped his pants, I wondered if either guy would say anything, like "thanks" or "really great job." Anything. They didn't. Once again, I saw the difference between men and women. While some men can have anonymous sex, most women have to be talked to before they'll consider sleeping with someone immediately. They have to be told for at least two hours they're hot and have to be taken out somewhere before they have sex.

After the gender fuck, I walked home by myself on the streets of New York City at 2 A.M., without fear. Until I went into a deli and experienced an attempted gay-bashing where four guys tried to pick a fight with me. Running out of there fast, I walked past an ex-boyfriend who didn't recognize me, then went over to my brother's, who took one look at me and exclaimed, "You look like my new ugly brother!"

After two days as a man, I really missed being a girl. It was difficult suppressing my femininity. I remember that as a child my mother begged me to be more "ladylike." (Look at me now.) On the other hand, it was a relief not to have my body parts evaluated on the streets of New York City. And the condescending attitude of superiority I sometimes elicit from men disappeared. Also, as as a reasonably attractive woman, I am used to being at least checked out by men. But as a short, ugly guy, I got no attention whatsoever from the opposite sex. There are no special privileges in being Mr. Regular. It is not true that women don't care about men's looks.

For me, the turn-on aspect of the gender facade was having the opportunity to flirt with gay men and have my flirtations returned. For the three gay women who became drag kings with us, their erotic experience was to adopt the male gaze and flirt with straight women who might not have flirted back if they knew these were gay women.

As my second day as a man came to a close, I went home and looked in the mirror once again. I visualized what it would be like having sex with the new me. I admired my masculine bulge and fondled my cotton balls. I got turned on by the man in the mirror. Then I did the most manly thing a horny guy could do. I had sex with myself.

WHIP IT good

Dominatrix for a Day

i've had my share of sexual requests, from the guy who wanted me to dress up like a harem girl in a veil to the one who asked me to dye my pubies pink. But recently I met someone who wanted me to dominate and humiliate him, walk him around in a dog collar, and make him lick the bowl.

When I first met Mr. Long-Haired Rock Guy, he didn't fit my stereotype of the wormy submissive I usually associate with the S&M crowd. After a number of late-night conversations, he made it clear to me that if the two of us went out, I would have to spank him, among other things. At first I thought he was kidding, until he said, "I don't want you to be my girlfriend, I want you to be my mistress."

I had no clue where to begin. I needed lessons, a class in Dominance 101. So I went back to school for some adult education at the Learning Annex, the venerable institution where they teach such courses as "How to Flirt" and "How to Talk to Your Cat."

The class I signed up for was called "Become a Dominatrix for Fun, Love, Profit—for Women Only—Take Control of Your Lover, Your Boss, Your Date."

Taught by Norwegian dominatrix Ava Taurel, Mistress Ava began by telling us that S&M is not "perverted" or "sick," instead calling it "sophisticated." "Once you try S&M, you will never want to go back to vanilla sex," she explained. Domination is about "rewards and pleasure," she continued. "You must relieve the submissive of the responsibility, get rid of the guilt." Many of her clients, she told us, are lawyers, Wall Streeters, and high-powered executives, men who have high-stress jobs who want to relinquish control. (In other words, powerful men who want sexy women in rubber fetish outfits to spank them like big babies.)

Standing in front of the classroom, Mistress Ava demonstrated spanking techniques on one of her slaves. As she spanked his bare butt, she narrated, "Spank! Then massage! Spank! Then massage!" Demonstrating with a big paddle with studs on it, she pointed out that "your paddle is one of the most important purchases you can make." Next she suggested some slave dialogue. "The slave should say something like 'I kneel before my mistress. I kiss her toes. She likes the cane.'"

Mistress Ava encouraged us to be imaginative. "Try ice cubes stuck on private parts! Or a cigarette tip on the nipples can be fantastic! It's an electrical thrill!" She also taught us that "Europeans are more advanced than Americans"—they use everything from Saran Wrap to clothespins, and they enjoy face slapping.

Then she went through the fetishes and fantasies, including feet ("Some men like the smell of sweaty feet. Make him really want your shoe") and bondage fantasies ("It's exciting for the slave to wear a mask, especially one with a breathing tube").

Sensory deprivation is an important aspect of S&M, and Mistress Ava suggested building up gradually "until you move into more advanced, 'heavy player' devices like head cages." Then she told the class, "Many men like to be smothered with parts of the body, such as the breasts." (*New York Post* head-line—CLEAVAGE KILLER: MAN SUFFOCATED BY 44D'S)

At the end of the class, she shared some tips on how to publicly humiliate someone: "Tell your slave to go out and buy the biggest box of Maxi pads he can find and stand with it in a big-hotel lobby."

Then she suggested dressing up our slaves in women's clothing ("Some men like the feeling of wearing women's panties. It makes them very erect"), then added that "cross-dressers might enjoy dildo rape."

When the class was over, she encouraged the one hundred or so students to mingle. My "women only" classmates consisted of a number of conservatively dressed women in power suits who looked like they needed to relax. One tall one asked me for my phone number and gave me her card. Her name was Frank.

After the course, I did some homework on the subject. I learned that ritual role-playing and theatrics are essential elements to S&M play and that humiliations suffered as a child (such as being paddled by a hot schoolteacher) can be twisted into sexual thrills as an adult. Also, they eroticize what scares them.

Now I was ready to apprentice with someone who could literally show me the ropes. I called a local S&M parlor and told the woman that I had a boyfriend who wanted to be dominated and I needed some lessons. I was told that for $150 and a $30 "membership fee" I could sit in on a session and maybe pick up a few tips on scrotal torture.

After I walked into Pandora's Box, a house of domination that was decorated like a fake eighteenth-century French salon and nicknamed the Disneyland of Domination for its themed rooms, I filled out a two-page form of preferences, a prenegotiated list usually filled out by submissives.

The dominatrix read me the list of "activities," which I had to rate from one to five in order of interest. In addition to the bread-and-butter stuff (spanking, "moderate to severe," and discipline), there was also flagellation, genital torture, infantilism, puppy training, foot slavery, teacher/student, boss/employee, hostage/captor, and prisoner/guard.

"Uniforms?" she asked sternly. "What kind do you like?"

"Nurse!" I blurted out, as if I were on a game show.

"Oh, that's a very popular one."

"What are the other ones?"

"A lot of men like Nazi."

Now there's a good one, I thought, really fun.

As I sat in a small waiting room, I waited for "Bob" and two of the mistresses who would train me. The receptionist told me that we were in luck—Bob is into public humiliation and wants me to watch. As I waited, I could hear another guy in the next room screaming at the top of his lungs, as if he were having an operation with no anesthesia. (He was paying $180 an hour for this.)

The first mistress, a sexy brunette with big lips and big hair, appeared in a skintight leopard bodysuit. She addressed me as "Mistress Anka" and showed me to the dungeon and medical room while the other mistress got Bob warmed up. While we were waiting, she said, real cranky, "Don't let me fool you that I do this for money. I like doing this. I'm a lifestyle mistress. This is not a nine-to-five job for me."

Then she asked, "Have you ever been tied up? To be dominant you have to also have tried the submissive role," she explained as I visualized myself tied up to the Catherine wheel for hours as it spun relentlessly. Then she showed me how to tie someone to the rack with leather restraints, and how to lock someone in "the human cage." "If he is a bad slave, you make him drink your urine," she said sternly. "For private clients I let them eat my shit, but that takes a day to prepare."

Next, she showed me how to dog-train a slave. "Make him go into the doghouse and eat real dog food," she said harshly. Then she showed me the torture devices in the drawer. "I like to put nipple clamps on the slave's eyelids . . . these weights are for scrotal torture. I've seen some guys who use these and they have really stretched-out balls, like elephant balls," she tells me, pronouncing *ball* "bawl." This was one tough New York chick. No, this chick was more than tough. She was a bitch. A professional bitch. I wondered what she was like with PMS.

She led me into the next room, a small schoolroom with a

blackboard, paddle, and dunce cap. Across from that was the medical "clinic," an all-white room straight out of a fifties B movie. "This is where the slave goes," she said, pointing to an operating table. "Here he can look up at the mirror and see how stupid he looks," she added with disgust.

Hanging on the wall was a white leather straitjacket next to a case housing a gas mask, a big rubber fist, catheters, speculums, and rubber gloves. "And here's some enema bags," she said as I felt a wave of nausea.

"So let me get this straight," I asked. "It's straitjacket first, enema bag second, and gas mask third?"

At that point, the other mistress summoned me to the dungeon, so I could practice on Bob. In crawled Bob on all fours, a balding, gray-haired man in his midfifties, naked except for a dog collar, being led on a leash by a French mistress. Something about six inches long told me that "Big Boy Bob" was being a naughty doggy.

After the two verbally tortured him, calling him "subhuman," the French mistress handed me a riding crop. "Be careful not to hit the kidneys," she warned as I wacked Bob's butt. Then, she handed me a cat-o'-nine-tails and showed me how to use it. ("It's all in the wrist," she told me.) As I repeatedly spanked, I couldn't help but feel ridiculous. "Yes, mistress," he grunted, his naked butt sizzling as I improved my technique. At this point it hit me that I was spanking a guy who looked like Frank Perdue. ("It takes a tough man to make a tender chicken.")

As I spanked, it occurred to me that I take way too much crap from men, probably because I'm too sweet. Now I was into it. This is when I let the crusty dude have it. This is also when I decided to change my name to Mistress Spanka.

After my session, I agreed somewhat with Mistress Ava's theory that it's the submissive who has the ultimate power. Bob worked my nerves so thoroughly that I gave him what he really wanted. But I wondered if I was cut out for this. Coming from an affectionate family, I had a hard time inflicting pain on someone else, even if he was enjoying it. S&M is about playing a role, toying with the exchange of power, and inflicting or receiving torture. It's about psychological tension and theater; it's kinky sex without the sex. With a professional dominatrix the only sex involved is the slave being "allowed" to end the session with his hand.

In S&M parlors, there is no emotional intensity, but if I got into S&M play at home, it could lead to sex and affection. Especially if my designated spankee turned me on. It was time to take Mr. Rock up on his offer of being my Slave Boy, then Mistress Anka would unleash and relieve him. And the reward for Mistress Anka would be sex with Slave Boy.

Just then, he called. I thought about the positive aspects of becoming a dominatrix (e.g., goddess worship, role reversal, not submitting to male power). I commanded him to come over.

Slave Boy arrived with the look of an excited puppy. It was time for puppy training. I put a dog collar around his neck, led him into the bathroom, and made him wait for me.

I put on the fishnets, the corsets, the gloves. For me, the sexiest part of being a dominatrix was getting to wear the outfit. I felt cartoony, like Wonder Woman with a whip.

When I let him out, I put a gag ball in his mouth and led him around my apartment for a while making him jump over things. He got instant dog wood.

Next, I handcuffed him to the bed, dropped hot wax on his nipple rings, and tried out my newly mastered whipping techniques. The harder I whipped and spanked, the more he grunted in ecstasy. Then I made him scrub my toilet bowl with a toothbrush. Seeing my porcelain bowl sparkle was a huge turn-on. I got hard.

The next day, Slave Boy called. He said he "liked to be used," that it excited him, that S&M is foreplay for him. When I asked him how his welts were, he said he wanted more. But I think once was enough; I don't exactly see myself making this a lifestyle. Besides, my wrist was sore and I had S&M elbow. But as far as Slave Boy and I were concerned, I knew "our relationship" was doomed when he told me, "You know, I was toying with the idea of mummification."

SEXCURSIONS

Regina Casagrande

V I V A L a ʃ g i r L ʃ

Road Tripping to Vegas

We were four wild girls in the wild, wild West. On the road. To Vegas. Sin City. We were out for kicks, in for trouble. We were a gang of four who wanted cheap thrills. We were Thelma and Louise, and Faster Pussycat, Kill! Kill! Cruisin' for action. Living for the moment. Looking for Zen, and the art of the foxmobile.

We were a pussy posse on wheels: Delilah, a tattoo artist, with an armload of ink and a chestful of silicone; 36DDs and proud of 'em. Sally, a film director and long-legged amazon, a man-eater, a heartbreaker. And Sky, a photographer and Harley drivin' "cooter on scooter" with weenie radar who can spot a hard-on ten miles away.

Sky drove first, I rode "seatcover" in the front, Sally and Delilah rode "bitches" in the back. First stop: 7-Eleven for road essentials. Cherry Big Gulps and "ribbed for her pleasure" condoms. As we passed a recreational vehicle filled with rednecks making blow-job hand gestures toward us, we agreed not to pick up hitchhikers, unless of course they looked like Brad Pitt.

As we passed a bunch of erect cacti and the Bun Boy restaurant, we started talking about men and how we like to use them as sex objects. One of the ho's in the car admitted she was into "sport fucking." This explains why she refers to every guy she goes out with as "the guy I'm having sex with." We all wondered how she introduces these guys at parties. ("This is Bob, my orgasm facilitator.")

After we pulled into the gas station and put the nozzle in our tank, the attendant started screaming at us, demanding that we pull out and up to the next pump, so "other people won't have to wait."

"Chill," we told him, "there's nobody behind us for miles."

That's when he called us "stupid females." We told him to bite us. He freaked and ran toward us, like he was ready to bet us up. Delilah pulled off her maxi pad, threw it out the window, and yelled, "Suck my Kotex!" As we peeled away, nozzle still in the tank, she yelled, "And while you're at it, get some front teeth!"

WELCOME TO LAS VEGAS the sign said as we hit town. As we drove down the strip of casinos and hotels with flashing lights and blaring signs, we passed the Frontier with fake fountains and waterfalls, and another hotel with two gigantic tiki heads in front. Stunned by the level of tackiness, Sky said, "I can't believe people think tons of huge, obnoxious signs are glamorous." Sally said, "I can't believe people with butts that big wear shorts that small."

Driving by dozens of wedding chapels with glittering lights (including a drive-in one), we realized that Vegas was a spiritual mecca and the perfect place for that memorable wedding. As we felt the love, we all got squishy and talked about our bridal dreams. Delilah wants to be wed by a televangelist. Sally wants to get married at the Liberace Museum. I decided on an Elvis impersonator for my husband and a reception at Nick's Onion Rings.

At the hypnotically tacky Stardust, we had our picture taken with a hunky Vegas showguy ($10), who let us feel him up ($0). The friendly bellhop told Sally he liked her stilettos and he told us that he liked women with four-inch heels to walk on his back.

Since Vegas is stacked with strip clubs for men, we asked where we could go for a little boylesque. The helpful cabdriver recommended the "Thunder From Down Under: Manpower Australia" show, then suggested a swingers' club where "the orgy action really heats up." Then he volunteered to escort us. Everyone in Sin City was so accommodating.

After this, we wondered what room service in this town was like; since prostitution is legal in Nevada, we wondered if we could order hookers with our dinner.

With signs that say CASH YOUR PAYCHECKS HERE, WIN BIG BUCKS, the casinos are magnets for losers hoping to get lucky. At the pseudo-Roman Caesars Palace, one guy wearing a squirrel-like toupee who told me he was "in the entertainment business" promised he would "take me wherever I wanted to go."

It was off to the Great Pyramids of Egypt (without him) at the Luxor, where Sky, Delilah, Sally, and I marveled at the sight of the glitzy gold lion beckoning us into the giant plastic pyramid.

Once inside, we were high-roller chicks with our own gambling system: Let's play blackjack over there because the dealer is giving me a girl boner. After ordering free drinks and throwing our money away, we decided that since we had lost our shirts, we might as well bare our titties. It was our postfeminist revue—lifting our tops and then yelling, "What the hell are you looking at?"

Flashing was a symbol of our female bonding, a femme high five. We were women's libbers of the nineties. We were women, hear us roar, watch us flash!

We took our act to the Mirage and the Frontier. We were asked to leave, not because we were flashing our golden nuggets, but because we were taking photos. One guy who caught our floor show popped his eyes out as if he'd hit the jackpot.

In the true way of Zen, we were shedding our desires. According to its teachings, satori (the enlightened state) can be achieved through pedestrian activities. Along our way, we enlightened pedestrians, heightening their awareness of female pulchritude, raising them to a higher consciousness of hooterness.

The next night, our booty patrol went cruising for hot

cowpokes. That's when we discovered that Vegas attracts a bizarre assortment of people dying to party. At the Debbie Reynolds Hotel and Casino, in no particular order, we mingled with a prosthetic-limb salesman who liked Sky, a band of plastic-tablecloth manufacturers who liked Delilah, and a toilet-bowl salesman from Idaho who liked me.

After that place, we thought we'd have better luck at the Hard Rock Cafe, which locals told us is a pickup scene. "Didn't I see your breasts in front of the lions at Luxor?" a raging surfer dude asked us. He understood. He knew we were a band of roving thrasher flasher chicks. He saw us the night before when we were exposing ourselves in the girlie mobile and within seconds a carpool formed around us like a circling wagon train. Considering that people pay $78 to see Debbie Reynolds prance around a stage, we were in the right town. Here, practically anything passes for great entertainment.

That night at the Hard Rock Cafe, we decided to see Seal only because his manager gave us five free tickets. Before the show started, I picked up a cute twenty-one-year-old. Halfway into the third song, he whispered into my ear, "Wow, man, this is really adult contemporary." Afterward, we were invited to the VIP lounge where Mr. Love Songs refused to have his photo taken with us. On the way out, we met Gary *(Diff'rent Strokes)* Coleman, who was thrilled for the photo op, because at his height, his face got sandwiched directly between our breasts.

The next night, we "took in a show." Don Rickles at the MGM Grand won out over Siegfried and Roy, the animal illusion act at the Mirage. We had front-row seats, but they crowded so many people together that we couldn't sit up straight. We laughed, we cried, at Rickles's super politically incorrect Polack and Mexican jokes. These were followed by insults to honeymooner couples and a bunch of enema jokes that went over big with the geriatric crowd. When Delilah and I got up to visit the powder room, Rickles pointed at us and screamed, "Look! A couple of hookers going out to look for some heavy action!"

He wasn't the only one who had this impression of us. In fact, the three questions we were asked most frequently in Vegas were "Are you tattoo models?" "Are you girls in a rock-'n'-roll band?" and "Would you come back to my hotel room for two hundred dollars?"

But we didn't care what people thought of us. We were pro-sex feminists. We knew that acting slutty and baring our boobs made us look more like hookers than members of a women's caucus.

At 4 A.M., totally wasted, we decided to take one last drive, this time to the car wash. As we drove through, we decided to give Vegas a final encore. Within seconds, we were showing off our auto parts. Delilah and Sally flashed their headlights, Sky gave dashboard bush, and I did pressed ham on the windshield. As we drove out, one of the shammy boys exposed his squeegee. After that, our spirits felt truly cleansed.

At the end of the road, it wasn't where we ended up that was important, it was the journey. We realized that baring our souls (and our knockers), opening our hearts (and our blouses), made us feel a oneness with each other and with nature. It was the peeing on the side of the road we did together, the flashing that bonded us together. We also realized that if any of our careers didn't work out as planned, we could always open up a topless car wash.

Guy Aroch

ANKA does Aspen

Snowboard and Snowjobs

Aspen, Colorado—"playground of the superrich" (according to Robin Leach), the superglamorous resort town where over fifty superstars have superhouses, and the place where Ivana Trump and Marla Maples almost bitch-slapped each other on the slopes. But it wasn't the thought of tacky celebrities in a ritzy resort with breathtaking scenery that drew me to Aspen. It was the thought of horny mountain men and high-altitude heavy breathing.

In the seventies, Hollywood stars escaped to Aspen for its cowboy landscape, privacy, and incredible skiing. That's when skiing became chic, and celebrity-seeking, coke-snorting yuppies descended on the town, to "do the scene," even though half of them didn't ski.

It was the era of gigolo ski instructors (who the locals refer to as "sleazies") who worked the wealthy women for big tips and casual sex. Sitting outside the Aspen Ski School on my first day in Aspen, I met one of those guys. He was about fifty years old; an oversexed Ken-doll/ski-bum "lifer" who tried to hit on me with the line, "Hi! Do I give private lessons? You bet!" This was the first sign that this might not be my scene. The second was seeing Regis Philbin prance by in a snowsuit.

After this sighting, I took the gondola, an enclosed lift, up to the top of Aspen Mountain. I was joined by two couples from Texas—two jock guys and their ex–Dallas Cheerleader wives, all wearing red snowsuits and snorting coke.

On their way down, the lift had to be stopped because two skiers got into a fistfight. That's when I looked down and saw one of the Texas men whose coke looked like it was kicking in; he was urgently pulling his snowsuit down, attempting to hide under a tree as he extruded a steamin' foot-long hot dogger.

After this breathtaking scenery, it was time for Après-Ski, the postski pickup scene that the Texans in the gondola told me was really great and "the place to be seen." Once inside, the Little Nell's parade of fashion was delightfully appalling. A number of women from Texas were wearing big ol' fur coats, coats so conspicuous that if they wore them in New York, they would be instantly spray-painted.

One woman with the most elaborate, fluffiest fur coat I've ever seen looked down her bad ski-jump nose job at me as she walked by. A second woman's tasteful outfit featured a gigantic purple fur coat with feathered Jose Eber hat and white cowboy boots. It was one piece of work after another. It was

Dynasty. Another woman did runway in the white sweater and slacks ensemble with pearls, white brimmed hat, and matching white dog. The place looked like a plastic-surgery convention: there were more lifts in the room than on the slopes.

The younger women were wearing the ubiquitous skin-tight ski pants I came to call "snatch huggers." One sexy ski bunny's pants were so tight and her lips so puffy I wondered if she had had a collagen labial beef-up.

After the fashion show, I walked down and saw three sweet Johnny Deep look-alikes with amusing facial hair carrying snowboards. As I stood there salivating over them, a man who had tried to pick me up inside approached me again. He was from L.A. and was sporting a yellow ski suit with big black zebra stripes. When he saw me looking at the three cuties, he said, "I don't much care for snowboarders." When I asked him why not, he said, "Well, for one thing, they don't dress very well."

That night everyone was gossiping about the big party of the evening, an extravagant bash thrown by one of the town's several billionaires. Last year's party, which brought together Aspen's "society set," reportedly cost $250,000. (It also reportedly had prostitutes in the hot tub.)

Since I wasn't on the guest list, I cordially invited myself. After being rejected by five scary security men, I resorted to sneaking in with one of the parking valets. Once inside I saw tasteful debs in little black dresses with their tuxedoed husbands and a bunch of ex-playboy guys from L.A. in their fifties with much younger women who looked like Marla Maples clones. Dotting the room were a number of Pamela Anderson wannabe's with boob jobs and matching lip implants. In fact, everyone's breasts were so perky that night, I was afraid their balloons might pop in the high altitude.

Making my way across the room, I walked by the "hired help," three women wearing see-through dresses with no bras or underwear, looking for the hot tub.

In the next room, I saw Diana Ross descended upon by a throng of hungry paparazzi, one of whom pushed me into an hors d'oeuvres table in his fury to snap a picture. One of the few gay men I met the whole time I was in Aspen scraped the dip from my elbow with a cracker and said, "It's deelish!"

Upstairs, I watched a suit from L.A. vacuum an entire mountain of powder up his nose. When he approached me, I asked him, "So what brings you to Aspen?" He said, "I'm here to get laid." Then he said, "Sure are a lot of great tits here tonight."

Downstairs, one of the Pamela Andersons got up on stage and sang a Marilyn Monroe rendition of "Happy Birthday, Mr. President," followed by a striptease. Since I'd crashed the party, the least I could do was introduce myself to the party's host, who was bombed. He grabbed my plastic skirt and said, "You know what I like! Cheap clothing!" Now I know what billionaires like: cheap clothing and expensive prostitutes.

The next day, I went to a snowboarding store where I met Heidi, a boardin' Betty who was also shopping and helped me pick out my unmatching shredder outfit. Then I went for my first snowboarding lesson with five other people who also kept falling down. The hardest part of snowboarding was actually getting back up, thanks to being strapped to a fiberglass board with bindings and cementlike boots.

Once I felt confident carving out turns, cruising down the mountain was orgasmic. I dug flying down the mountain with white stuff flying in my face.

That night I met Heidi for dinner and she helped me pick up a hot snowboarder guy with muscles and long black hair that made him look like an American Indian Fabio. As he walked by the restaurant, we waved at him through the window, blowing kisses, and giggling like complete idiots. When he put his face up to the window, we invited him in (this technique would never work in New York).

On my fourth day in Aspen, but only my second day on the slopes, I went snowboarding with Alex, who offered to give me "private lessons." On the chairlift we were screaming because the powder looked so sweet. He kissed me on the cheek and I was so moved by the beautiful scenery that I let my tongue snowboard down his throat.

The skiers and shredders in Aspen hate each other. Skiers, who think they rule the slopes, like being comfortable and prosperous and are convinced they are superior; they think snowboarders have a bad attitude, no money, and no manners. Snowboarders think skiers are obsessed with money, are anal retentive, and suck.

After our gnarly run, we went to "do the scene" at the snowboarder version of après-ski—a woody bar plastered with girl graffiti such as "I saw Michael Bolton on Bunny Hill and his hair looked really bad" and "I did the men's room at Aspen Highlands."

The next day, Alex and I took a tour of the town in the Ultimate Taxi, a ridiculously souped-up cab covered with blinking lights. Inside, it was disco on wheels, with spinning mirrored ball, fog machine, and a microplane attached to the dashboard. We asked for the anti-establishment tour, which our disco driver obliged us with by cruising us past the psychedelic mushroom house, where ex-Playboy bunny Barbi Benton lived, a large tepee-shaped house with a gigantic middle finger on the roof.

Back at the romantic Hotel Lenado, Alex did the rustic mountain-man thing and built a fire. Despite the tacky tourists, what I liked most about Aspen was its earthiness. And, at that moment what I liked most about Aspen was Alex. Especially when he addressed me in his New Orleans drawl as "darlin'," a first for the urban Anka. As the flames crackled and I played with his hair, he hugged me and told me how I needed a man who would be sweet to me. I admitted I hadn't experienced that in a while. Then we talked about the Zen of snowboarding. Apparently, either the conversation or the fire got him hot, because he took off his shirt. Howdy six-pack! Then I took my shirt off and introduced him to "Anka's darlin's." Suddenly, our conversation shifted to the "pure physicality" of snowboarding. Things started to snowball. I was overcome with an avalanche of passionate kisses. It was a total meltdown. As the windows fogged up, I felt a ski pole rub against my leg and then knock on the door of my warm love lodge.

Sex on the Riviera

My fantasies of the glamorous Cannes film festival took me riding breathless on a Vespa with Jean-Paul Belmondo, absorbing myself in smoky conversation with a romantic Frenchman, and if I got lucky, having two men, à la *Jules and Jim,* fall madly in love with me. I would attend stimulating screenings by day and lavish parties by night. I would meet movie stars and interesting directors with weird glasses.

The festival du film prides itself on a history of promoting "art house" films. But as soon as I arrived, all I saw were posters for sexploitation B movies such as *Headless Body in Topless Bar, Cat Girls in Heat* (who invent man-killing Kitty Litter), and *Lap Dancer* ("from the producers of *The Forbidden Dance* and introducing the 'Lap Rap'"). As a lover of all genres of cinema, I was bummed that Troma Pictures had no screening for *Attack of the 60-Foot Centerfold.* I wondered what it would be like to have a six-inch clitoris.

On my first afternoon in Cannes, I soaked up some mise-en-scène. I watched Sharon Stone in a ball gown with nine tuxedoed bodyguards climb the red-carpeted steps of the Palais theater to promote her movie. Then it was off to a walk on the beach where I watched the Miss Cannes contestants whipping off their bikini tops to promote their breast implants. (The festival du breastiful.) I watched the packs of paparazzi strapped with gigantic, penis-shaped lenses combing the shores looking for anyone famous, topless, or preferably both. Ever since Brigitte Bardot took her top off in 1957 to promote *And God Created Woman,* the tradition continues, with always a few women thinking that if they take their tops off for the paparazzi, they will be discovered by a major director. In reality, they end up being discovered by *Juggs* magazine.

The next day I went to a screening of an Australian film, *Sex Is a Four-Letter Word.* Ten minutes into the movie, a man sat next to me. As I'm watching the film, his jacket rubbed my thigh. I pushed it away. Then I felt something between my legs. His fingers were rubbing my croissant. This is when I wished I had my French phrase book with me so I could look up "Could you keep your greasy French paws off my vagina?"

After my molestation, I went to the beach again. As I'm lying on my stomach, surveying the shore for male derriere and thinking how unfair it is that women are going topless but men aren't going bottomless, a Roman Polanski look-alike walks by, pulls down his bathing trunks, and waves his baguette at me, then runs up and grabs a handful of my butt.

After two petite molestations in one day, I was beginning to think this was a quaint French custom.

Every night there was a big party promoting a different film, many behind the big hotels on the beach. (Anyone wearing shorts was denied entrance by the French fashion police.) Thousands of people showed up at these parties, some spending the whole day trying and failing to get invitations. One of the few ways to crash these parties was to have a huge yacht anchored offshore, like the group of swinging Middle Eastern billionaire guys in white linen suits with hot-looking women on their arms who crashed the MTV party in small launch boats. Since the women were much taller, much younger, and much better looking than the men they were fawning over, I couldn't tell whether they were models or call girls. Okay, I'll have to go with call girls. One of the guys told me he had 60 brothers and 45 sisters. He said that last year all 105 children met at his father's house because not all of them had met their father. For some reason, I said, "You know, I'd really like to try on one of those veil things." He got really excited and asked, "Could I take your picture wearing one?" I envisioned myself in a Saudi Arabian porno magazine called *Veils and Tails*.

As I watched Tina Turner get chased by a throng of paparazzi, I started talking to some French guys. Of course, I went for the one who spoke absolutely no English. His friend translated, "He loves you. He thinks you are sweet." "The Frenchmen are so romantic," I start thinking. After about twenty minutes of hearing how much his friend has fallen deeply in love with me, I am feeling la stimulation. "He wants to make love to you," says his friend. "On the beach. In ten minutes." I was definitely tempted. A little sex on the Riviera sounded good. I even had the fantasy of the three of us in bed together, his friend translating things like "Jacques says he wants you to do it a little to the left."

At this point, Angela, a journalist I met on the plane, walked by. I asked if she would, in my position, speak the language of love. "Dance with him first," she suggested. So we danced. One dance and I knew that if he made love the way he danced, I was in for l'ejaculation rapide.

The next night I went to a nightclub and flirted with a guy who, how you say, was le hot stuff, a handsome architect who designed villas in Nice. And he could dance. We made a date for the next night. When he picked me up, he brought two other guys. (Threesomes and foursomes were becoming a running theme in Cannes.) For three hours—on a drive through town, during drinks in a café, and while on a walk on the promenade, I entertained his two friends while he talked the entire time on a cellular phone. I contemplated getting his attention by calling him from the corner phone booth, but figured he would put me on hold. Finally, he had time to squeeze me in and suggested we go back to my hotel, "to make love." When I told him to drop me off at the club instead, he told me he couldn't be seen with me because his wife lives in Cannes. My romantic date had turned into a tragic French film, my nomination for this year's Palme d'Or award: *Sex, Lies, and Cellular Phone.*

The next two days I would spend at the Hot d'Or ceremonies with the international porno film crowd, an event Michael Douglas said "brought down the whole spirit of the film festival," which made me want to attend even more.

At the oceanside luncheon, I sat next to the formerly penisless John Wayne Bobbitt, now a porno actor, and his manager, who told me about John's line of products including overnight penis shields. When I asked John what his most frequently asked questions were, he said, "How's it hangin'?" "Didn't it hurt?" and "Why didn't you kill the bitch?" When I asked him what he thinks of breast implants, he said, "Well, at first they are good for a girl's esteem. But then they can corrupt a girl's character and she could become conceited." Then he added, "I'm getting a penis enlargement."

At the table next to us were six porno girls who between them represented about two tons of silicone fun. ("Table for six, please, and could you bring some high chairs for our breasts?") Other porno actresses were with their *Star 80*–type boyfriend/managers, who followed them around handing out press releases. One porno star wanna-be told me she was up for an award for her gang-bang movie. "I had sex with five guys," she explained, "but it was okay because my boyfriend was one of them." Another said she does only girl-girl films because her boyfriend would get mad if she cheated on him with another guy. A third told me she sometimes brings girls that she meets on the set back to her husband because "you know how guys love that."

Next I talked to porno legend Randy West, who told me he has done over eight hundred films in his career. When I asked him what he does when he's having a hard time keeping it up on the set, he said, "I flash back to my days as a male stripper, the early eighties, when I went to a bachelorette party and did the bride's sister, the bride, and the mother of the bride."

At the Hot d'Or ceremony the next night, awards were given out for achievements like Best Box Cover and Best Gang-Bang Video. (Does the whole gang accept the award?) As people won for things like Best New Starlette, presenters and winners cheerily fondled each other's butts as they accepted their awards. An honorary award went to John Wayne Bobbitt. "When his wife cut his sex off," read the badly translated program, "he didn't know that one day he would be acting in a porno movie and change his misfortune to happiness."

Accepting the award, he began, "You know, there's nothing worse than waking up in the morning and losing your penis." Then he thanked his doctor ("Without him I would be dead") and his best friend, who drove him to the hospital. I wondered if he would be thanking the road crew for retrieving his organ.

At the party afterward, Bobbitt's manager (who was literally managing his meat) asked me if I wanted to see it. ("Bobbitt means 'beautiful penis' in French," his manager told me.) "Sure, I'll take a look at it," I said as John led me into the john. It wasn't exactly beautiful, but it appeared fairly normal except for the ragged scar around the base. As we walked out of the stall, a hot porno guy teased, "Hey, Anka, now that John showed you his, let's see yours!" Considering I was in the men's room at an X-rated awards ceremony, I stuck out my butt and struck some porno poses. Out of the woodwork appeared John "Buttman" Stagliano, the Russ Meyer of butts, whose films include *Bend Over Babes* and *Butt Freak*. "I got into film," he told me, "because I'm into butts." Then he said, "I'm especially turned on to assholes."

"I have that same problem," I told him.

Just then, my horny porny pal Randy West walked in and invited me to join him on the set of a movie he is going to direct. Being a consenting adult, I bent over and said, "I'm ready for my close-up, Mr. DeMille."

мerry XXXMAS

Hometown for the Holidays

each year as Christmas season approaches, I look forward to going home and visiting my parents. This is when I get a chance to return to our version of family values. My parents, who are open-minded and liberal, had permissive attitudes toward child rearing (look at the result). We are a cross between *The Addams Family* and *The Cosby Show*. Maybe we should get our own sitcom.

Since we are not a conventional family, we do not partake of the usual Christmas ceremonies such as tree trimming and holiday decorating. We do, however, have our own special rituals. My mother, a former opera singer, prefers the theatrical aspect of looking into other people's windows. After Christmas dinner we don mother-and-daughter black turtlenecks and ski masks, wait until it gets dark, and then

Andrew Brusso

walk around the neighborhood peering into people's dining rooms.

Part of going home for the holidays is catching up on the small-town news. My mother, who enjoys clipping articles from the local paper for my amusement, saves such choice articles as the "Nude Man Flings Beef" story about some drunk, naked guy with underwear on his head who got arrested for flinging slabs of meat at people's windshields.

Next, I read front-page stories about the closing of the

massage parlor for giving "manual releases" and about the married head of the local bank who was arrested when they raided the local X-rated video store and caught him in a booth being serviced by a seventeen-year-old boy through a hole in the wall.

Because I view these holiday visits as free psychological counseling, I always discuss everything in my life with my parents, including love and sex. After I unload my most recent traumas, Dad, a sensitive and evolved man, always gives me new books on feminism and then tells me his latest penis jokes. ("What does a man with a nine-inch penis have for breakfast? Well, this morning I had . . .")

Dad, a retired corporate executive who apparently misses the office, wears a suit and tie twenty-four hours a day. Since this is a seven-day-a-week outfit, my brother and I have come to the conclusion that he has a surgically implanted prosthetic tie. (He has been spotted by neighbors cutting the grass with a tie on.) Around the house Dad sports the Teddy Kennedy look: jacket, tie, and boxer shorts. When the doorbell rings, Dad always says, "Wait a minute while I put my pants on!" forcing visitors on the other side of the door to draw their own conclusions as to why he isn't wearing any.

Last Christmas Eve, Dad, Mom, and I made the mistake of answering the door to a group of local Jesus freaks ebulliently singing Christmas carols. They didn't seem to notice that Dad was standing at the door with no pants, although one of the carolers looked at him as if she thought he might flash her. By the third chorus of "Jingle Bells," the carolers, who couldn't sing worth shit, were working our nerves. (Mom, do you have those apples with the razor blades in them left over from Halloween?) After a few more torturous minutes of holiday purgatory we pretended we were Jewish.

The small-town American mentality provides hours of amusement for my family and friends, and so an essential part of the home ritual is a tour of this Maryland town of forty thousand. (Think of a slightly Southern Twin Peaks.)

First we drive by the Fountain Head Country Club golf course, where at fifteen I lost my virginity on the seventeenth tee and found a new use for the ball-washing machine. Next we stop at the 7-Eleven, where the local inbreds in pickup trucks yell, "Hey, faggots!" to all the men in our car.

Then I drive by my local high school, where I point out such important landmarks as the parking lot where I was felt up for the first time in the backseat of a car. Conveniently located next door is the Kaufman Medical Center, where fifteen-year-old girls went to obtain birth control devices. A few blocks down is the apartment complex where a couple of teachers lured my girlfriend and me back to, got us drunk on whiskey sours, and put the moves on us. (At fifteen, we looked twenty-five.)

The tour ends with a drive by the county jail, where my father had to bail me out twice. After the second time, to keep me out of trouble, he suggested we confine the party to our house. This is when the Rad residence turned into party central with the basement functioning as an underage drinking and make-out den to which I invited the town's most attractive juvenile delinquents.

My parents have always encouraged me to bring my boyfriends home for the holidays. My mother, who has a fondness for romance and *la passióne,* always finds these holiday visits entertaining. My father's motivation, on the other hand, is to check out the latest creep

To this day, my family likes meeting my suitors. My mother mixes martinis and tells the guy how cute he is, while my father subtly asks for his résumé. My mother always hopes he's marriage material, while my father always hopes he's not.

Meanwhile, my brother, a sculptor, thinks it's his job to psychoanalyze every boyfriend I bring home. He somehow managed to get one boyfriend to reveal that he could suck his own penis by wedging himself up against the toilet bowl. Jim's psychiatric evaluation: "obsessive-compulsive wanker." Other nicknames for my former boyfriends have included "psycho," "dildo," "loser," and "moron." Usually, my father politely acts as if he likes my boyfriends. The only man who ever met with his genuine approval was my college boyfriend. Dad thought he was great; intelligent and funny. Mom thought he was dreamy; handsome and charming. Two weeks after graduation he dumped me. Shortly afterward he announced he was gay.

When it comes to sleeping arrangements, my parents have no problem letting us kids sleep in the same room with our holiday honeys. However, one Christmas while we were all having breakfast, my brother's then girlfriend started tonguing him in midpancake and dragged him into his bedroom, transforming our house into a love hotel. Hearing his sex-starved girlfriend yelling "Oh, Jimmy!" a million times through the air-conditioning ducts made my mother and me lose our appetites.

I'm for overhearing everyone (or anyone) having sex—

everyone but my brother or my parents. After a few more barnyard squeals, my mother and I jumped into the car and went to the mall to buy new sheets and earplugs.

Meanwhile, Dad just sat there, finished his Wheaties, read the paper, and listened contentedly with the same proud look on his face that he had when Jim scored a touchdown in junior high. Afterward he said, "Good job, Son."

Today, each time I bring someone home and we head out for some local nightlife, just to be goofy Dad sticks his head out the front door as we're pulling out of the driveway and yells, "Call me from the police station!"

WIN a Date

Joseph Pluchino

► With Anka

w i N - a - D A T E i —
t H e c o N t e ʃ t

Stiff Competition

i'll do anything for my readers, even date them, which is why I decided to hold the Win-a-Date with Anka Contest. At first I was worried: two days before the official deadline, only a few entries had dribbed into my male bag. Then suddenly I was flooded with over a thousand entries from eligible bachelors. I was ready to select my dream date, my mystery man, the new Mr. Anka.

Immediately disqualified were entries that smelled, letters with no photo, or letters with guys posing with strippers. Also eliminated were letters like the one that said, "I am an introvert. I have no friends. I stay in my room a lot."

I had to agree with one contestant, Dave from Raleigh, North Carolina, who wrote, "Normal people would never do this." As I began to open the first pile of letters, the demographics of my appeal were starting to shape up: eight virgins, two cross-dressers, and a bunch of guys in prison.

Although the contest rules stated, "To put yourself in the running, write an essay and describe yourself," it was the physical descriptions that piqued my interest. Among my favorites were "I'm white but I really do have rhythm," "I'm black and I really do have a large penis," "I am a three-speed vibrating manservant," and "My genitals are encased in Lucite"(?). A number of contestants mentioned their butts as assets worth telling me about. A cartoonist from Texas told me, "The *Buns of Steel* video really paid off." Andre, a twenty-five-year-old from Costa Mesa, California, boasted, "My best feature is my butt, which to everyone's amazement can hold a credit card when properly clenched." I would really be amazed if he could take money out of an ATM without using his hands.

Many sent in photos, including expired gym cards, driver's licenses, old prom photos, and five-year-old graduation shots. One guy sent in a photo of himself breaking into someone's house with a crowbar. Another sent one of himself sitting on the toilet.

Reasons why people wished to win a date included, "I'm stuck in the Midwest and I need out! The people here are inbred, so I don't date." Another entrant said, "I haven't had a date since '88."

Several people sent in a list of reasons why I should go out with them, ranging from "I've been waiting to meet you all my life" to "Embarrassing gas problems of childhood all cleared up." One guy simply put, "Because I'm huge." Mick G. tried to impress me with his career in "cat yoga" and enclosed a photo of himself and a cat wearing turbans. Others tried compliments, always an effective technique. Michael, a soccer player, said, "I like your Fellini-esque approach to crotch matters." A thirty-two-year-old songwriter became an instant semifinalist with the sentence "It turns out that cunnilingus is one of my favorite acts."

The question "How would you spend the big dream date?" prompted one entrant to describe what he would do *before* the date: "Practice lines, eat oysters, shave genitalia." Another guy thought it would be fun to "Drive around until we saw a HOT DONUTS sign flash on." A photographer suggested we go to Memphis and "see the great old mighty Graceland, home of the amphetamine King, where we could photograph each other lying limp by the toilet with various pills on the floor." That could be good.

Not surprisingly, to many the Win-a-Date with Anka Contest meant Win-a-Lay with Anka. Many answered "Tell me how you would spend your dream date" with some variation on a picnic basket, champagne, and my legs up in the air. This was especially true for the virgins who wrote in. Many said they were late bloomers. (The contest rules said, "Must be twenty-one.") One twenty-two-year-old wrote a five-page letter describing how I would deflower him, chronicling every step of the process. To close, he wrote, "Afterward, if you are hungry, I will take you to Denny's."

Others thought it was the Win-a-Date with the Other Woman Contest. "I *sort* of have a girlfriend," confessed Lincoln, a thirty-year-old philanderer from New York City, "and I feel a little guilty writing this. She is a sexy woman. She gets wet when we are driving or having phone sex. Thank God I met her, but I would still see you, Anka." (Thanks for thinking of me, Lincoln.) Another man, Bobby from Iowa, who is married *and* dating, sent in a photo of himself with his wife and kids. His idea of the dream date: the wife and kids climb up the Statue of Liberty, he climbs in my bed.

In addition to my manly suitors, I also received a few entries from women. One self-described "lesbo-girl" informed me, "You don't know what you are missing." A second suggested we could go out and "dis sniffing breeders." A third, who lived in NYC, said, "I'm into red bras and latex stockings," then added, "Of course I'd wait for the second date for leather garter belts and nipple clamps."

Most entertaining were the video dates. One from Greg, a twenty-two-year-old burgeoning filmmaker who used a female friend to enact what our date would be like: pulling my bra off, getting into the shower with me, getting on top of me, and finally, combing my wet hair before flossing our teeth.

The most dramatic was the "auto-asphyxiation" video sent courtesy of Ronald, whose idea of a great date was hanging himself from the rafters and masturbating. Another killer video was from Chris in Missouri, who dressed up like a total hick and said things like "I would let you perform your duties as a woman, as I see fit. I need to take you out of that freak show they call New York."

One contestant actually dropped off his entry in person when I was in San Francisco. He was a six-foot-five guy with bright green hair and tattoos bearing roses and a raspberry smoothie, proclaiming himself the "biggest freak in San Francisco" (impressive!). Juiceboy's audiotape said stuff like "I want to drive you around in a '76 Olds station wagon. I want you to boss me around." He became a semifinalist.

I was flattered by everyone who made the effort to enter the contest because, let's face it, I'm not exactly a prize. In the end, ten semifinalists touched my metaphorical button; I'm treating all of them to a preliminary phone date. The winner will receive an all-expenses-paid trip to New York and a possible chance at getting lucky. Choosing the winner will be difficult because I know it will be a toss-up between contestants like Brett from Florida, who wants to take me "on an adventure which will awaken the senses, thus setting off the race toward sedentary lifestyles, contemporary ennui, and the dominator society," and the dude who wants "to walk around New York in Kiss boots." Or will it be the guy who wants a horse-and-buggy "Amish date," where I wear "a bonnet, black cape, and prayer veil"? Or Scott from San Diego, who suggests we "steal a car and drive to Vegas, in a fit of wild, born-again, coming-of-age type abandon while wearing each other's underwear"? I just can't decide. . . .

WiN-a-DATE ii—
tHe dreaM date

San Francisco

after opening almost a thousand entries from my beloved Win-a-Date contestants, I still wasn't convinced I had found the new Mr. Anka. But suddenly, there he was, a twenty-seven-year-old student from San Francisco who fell out of a Federal Express envelope and into my wet lap. One look at his photo and I was convinced he was my type, not that I really *have* a type. Since I'm not that superficial, however, his letter was more crucial. "Ah, Dearest Anka," it began. "Angel of my subscription, light of my light reading, jewel of my mailbox. How 'bout a date?"

So far his mojo was working. "*Anka über alles.* Sometimes women are jaded by their experiences with the average caveman," the letter began, holding my interest for the next four pages. By the end, I had received a number of compliments, found out that he liked real, assertive, intelligent, and sexy women, and learned that he read "Baudelaire, Bataille, Bowles, and Bukowski, and that's just the B's."

In addition to being intrigued by his self-description ("the earnest young romantic—you know, the one with the flowing swashbuckler shirt and the crumpled flower"), I also liked his confession that he had had a "Bon Jovi 'fro" in junior high, which he described as "the ultimate embarrassing hairstyle."

Out of all the entries, it was clear that Tom* was my future dream date. I called to tell him he was the winner. "So I won, huh?" he said. "Do I get an appliance or anything?"

Luckily, we seemed to have an instant rapport, because a half hour into the conversation he called me "baby" and told me I sounded spicy. I said he sounded supertangy. He asked me what kind of perfume I wore and I said Airwick solid. He said he enjoyed the fresh pine scent of those rearview-mirror air fresheners. I think we were clicking.

Our conversation the next night, which included our philosophies of life and psychological analyses of other people, ended three hours later with his playing the guitar for me, prefacing his performance with "Promise you won't laugh."

As our last conversation descended into "What are you wearing?" but before it turned into phone sex, we made a date for San Francisco to be continued in New York if we could still stand each other.

He picked me up in my hotel lobby, we took one look at

*The real Win-a-Date's name has been changed.

each other, and after nine hours of conversation on the phone, we were both suddenly at a loss for words, like a couple of fourteen-year-olds trying to pretend we weren't nervous. "You look great," he stammered. He was hot: black hair, blue eyes, sideburns, earrings, and a bad-boy smile. "You look even cuter than your photo," I blurted out, sounding way too much like Marcia Brady.

In the car he had a cigar box filled with fresh-picked daisies. Just as men have simple needs (i.e., blow jobs), women love simple gestures of male gentleness.

We went to dinner and drank a bottle of wine and intoxicated each other. Instead of trying to impress each other with our résumés, we skipped the yuppie shit and moved right into the more earthy "You're so hot and I feel squishy" phase. We lavished compliments on each other ("I like the way your lips are shaped, I dig your layers . . ."), flirted, and stared into each other's eyes. We were like two zoned-out Moonies. We lost our appetites. We made the waitress nauseous.

After drinks and mild groping, we drove up to the phallic-looking Coit Tower ("Coitus Tower"), where we saw a bunch of couples making out. Unlike most of my first dates, Tom did not force the big one on me immediately, but instead gave me a piggyback ride and whisked me back to my hotel.

The next day, we decided to do a road trip, driving north to Calistoga in the Napa Valley where the hot springs are. First we drove up to Berkeley, then went to a flea market, where we bought aphrodisiacs from a woman who told us that her son "had an erection for three days using this stuff." We planned on using the aphros, but didn't need to, because

Tom seemed to have the same constant-erection problem the woman's son had.

As we drove through the lush countryside, we stopped in a forest so I could see the redwoods. To show me how sensitive he was, Tom hugged a tree. To show my appreciation, I hugged his woodie.

After dinner, we went back to our Victorian hotel for some "simple relaxation," the motto of Dr. Wilkinson's hot springs. I admit I wanted to date-rape Tom, but he said he wanted to wait, that he wanted to savor me, that I was special, and that he didn't want to have sex with me too soon. So we fooled around and fell asleep in each other's arms. (Later when I told my girlfriends, they thought he sounded romantic. My mother thought he sounded sweet. My gay friends thought he sounded gay. Tom's friends thought he sounded insane.)

The next morning it was time for us to experience Dr. Wilkinson's famous mud baths. We ordered "the works," which consisted of a mud bath, mineral bath, sauna, and massage. As we shelled out sixty-nine dollars each, I looked at the sign that mentioned "colonics" and made Tom ask how much those were. When the woman told us they don't do those anymore, we acted pissed that we couldn't get an internal cleansing.

As Tom went to the boy's side and I to the girl's, I found my dream date now consisted of me sitting alone in a tub of volcanic ash, mineral water, and peat moss that smelled like cow manure. An attendant put a shower cap on my head and mud on my face (I was looking good). Apparently, people enjoy this.

Meanwhile, Tom was on the other side talking to Dr. Wilkinson, who kept asking him if he had to pee before he stepped into the mud bath. (He could have pooped in there and nobody would have noticed the difference.)

Once I had my detoxifying mud bath, I couldn't wait to take a shower. I looked south to see huge clumps of mud stuck to my pubes. If I'd thrown some seeds on there, I would have sprouted a Chia Pet.

Afterward, we walked back to the hotel and offered to pick mud from each other's butts. Then we played around with the camcorder, Tom doing Brooklynese in his underwear. After this, we checked out and drove through the Napa Valley for a picnic in a vineyard. As we sat between the vines, I fed my dream date cherries. Then he kissed me, dripping and drooling the juice all over my neck, arms, and chest. After five minutes, I was covered in juice and dirt. I relished the moment big time. I offered him a slice of cherry pie.

At that point, he went to "get something from the car." Feeling sexy, earthy, and ripe, I lay in the vineyard and contemplated nature. But as nature always does, it reared its ugly head. I touched my forehead and felt a gigantic festering pimple, compliments of the "rejuvenating facial mask" that was supposed to "leave the skin supple and glowing." Back at the car, Tom was applying hydrocortisone cream to an acute attack of eczema on his hand. But in spite of our skin problems, the vineyard setting left us in a romantic mood, and I gave Tom a wine tasting from my jugs.

Our dream date came to a close, and as we drove back to San Francisco, I was feeling frisky and Tom was practically driving the car with his nasty thing. I didn't want the date to end. But unfortunately, I had to catch a flight in an hour. It was his idea to keep the sexual tension going; after all, it wasn't Win-a-Hump with Anka. And the fact that we didn't go all the way made it even sweeter and more exciting. The result was a case of blue balls for Tom and a case of swollen labes for me. "Hey, when I come to New York, can we totally shave each other?" he asked.

"I'll do whatever you want, baby."

"I'll do it right back."

For once, I'd picked a winner.

WiN-a-DATE iii —
tHe ƒequeL

New York

ƒor two weeks after that kissey face weekend, our love connection continued. Since Tom lived three thousand miles away,
we resorted to phone conversations, many of which began
with "What are you wearing?"

Considering that my winner had never been to New York
before, I sent him a ticket to continue our dream date. He
sounded excited. Literally. "I'm not going to play with myself
for a week," he told me. Statements like this were leading indi-
cators that whoopee in my party zone was imminent.

Since we never finished our game of "Where's the beef?"
in San Francisco, we put that on our New York itinerary. And
because Tom was so romantic and complimentary, telling me
over the phone I was "fine," "fly," and a "sexy mama," I said
he could stay at my apartment.

After dinner the first night, we went back to my place. "I'm old-fashioned," he told me as he passed out on my bed. I wasn't sure whether he was being romantic or a eunuch. The next night, as we got ready for bed, he told me his "balls hurt." By the third sexless night, I wondered if at the end of his ten-day visit he would have a top-ten list of "reasons why I don't want to have sex with Anka." Most guys will say anything to get into a woman's pants, yet he was saying anything to *not* get in mine.

Suddenly the passion had ended, the kisses were gone, the boner thing was over. Since he'd acted like Fabio and was all over me in San Francisco, I wanted to know what was going on. He explained that the day before his flight, his girlfriend had dumped him for her ex and that he was heartbroken (that meant he had a girlfriend in San Francisco when we were dream-dating). Then he told me he thought I wanted "emotional involvement," that I was "pressuring him," that I had "expectations," and that I "wanted love from him, blah, blah, blah." Little did he know, all I wanted from him was his penis for about an hour.

In San Francisco, he told me everything a woman ever wanted to hear, and now he was telling me everything I didn't. That afternoon, Tom looked upset and left to take a walk. There, sitting on his backpack, staring me in the face, was his journal. (Okay, so I had to hunt a little, but really, I'm not a snooper.) I knew he must have written something about me and I had to see what it was.

To my shock, there it was: "I'm tripping out on Anka. If I don't want to sleep with her, I'm not going through the motions." Then why was he here? Then it went on, "I don't owe her anything. She bought the ticket because she likes me." Then he said, "Anka is so into me, it pushes me away."

A few minutes later, Tom returned and told me, "I'm not physically attracted to you." This is when I considered the idea that maybe $20,000 worth of plastic surgery might not be such a bad investment after all.

Right after I received this news, my friend Carolyn came over to pick us up for a party. While she talked to him, I went to the bathroom and put a bag over my head.

Dazed and confused, I took Tom to the roof party. As soon as we arrived, he began ignoring me and started introducing himself to all my friends, especially my most attractive girlfriends, many of whom were there with their boyfriends. That's when he told me I was being "clingy." Then he said, "I need space." If I gave him any more space, we would have needed walkie-talkies.

As I watched him work the crowd and collect phone numbers, I thought about his entry letter, where he quoted something I had said in the *San Francisco Chronicle*: "Dating is a constant process of humiliation." He wrote, "I was touched by your sad confession."

Needless to say, my Win-a-Date was on the rocks. My dream date had turned into a nightmare. The rooftop party had also become a play where I watched the drama unfold: the wonderful Dr. Jekyll turns into the horrible Mr. Hyde. Then he finds me increasingly repulsive by the minute. By the end, he rejects me.

As he social-climbed, I stood there thinking, one thousand

letters and this is what I picked. Now I understand why people on *Love Connection* let the audience choose their dates. I should have blindfolded one of the guys in the mailroom and let him pick someone for me. I couldn't have done any worse. In fact, virtually anyone could have done a better job than I did.

Back at my bachelorette pad, we got into a fight. He told me my behavior "bugged" him. He said the way I "stared at him" at the party "irritated" him. Then he told me he wanted to be "just friends" and "hang out." If I would have known that, we could just have been pen pals. I used to be offended when someone used me just for sex, but now I was getting dumped without even getting humped.

At this point, I tallied up who won what. Tom: hundreds of dollars' worth of wining and dining in San Francisco, a plane ticket to New York, a limo from the airport, free accommodations, free drinks, two dinners, social contacts, a $100 "loan," and a head the size of those gigantic balloons in the Macy's Thanksgiving Day Parade. Anka: jack shit and a touch of low self-esteem.

Even after all this, my "winner" still thought he could crash at my place and talk about his possible future as a writer. I told him he had to leave my apartment and stay with his friends. If that wasn't possible, I volunteered to book him in a hotel (on Forty-second Street, making sure it was one of those with hourly rates and a bulletproof window at the front desk).

In our last romantic moments together, he shook my hand, said he still wanted to be "friends," and wanted to know if we could get together for coffee. Then, since he said he only had $26 for another week in New York, I gave the now ex–Mr. Anka a $40 alimony payment. As I shoved him out the door, I said, "Oh, sorry I wasn't attractive enough for you," to which he responded, "It wasn't just your looks, it was also your personality." Still looking for encouragement, he started picking my brain for career advice. Apparently, he saw the Win-a-Date contest as a career seminar. I suggested a job as a gigolo on the French Riviera.

SEXTREMES

Eline Mugaas

ƒLex aNd tHe
SINGLE GIRL

Getting Pumped at the
Mr. Olympia Contest

'm in heaven. A Hercules-like superman lifting his gigantic biceps steps through a cloud of smoke. He is wearing a bikini thong. He flexes his buns of steel. He poses. He smiles. Soon he is joined by thirteen other Über men who line up and strut their manly beefcake. I am not dreaming. I am at the Mr. Olympia contest, "The Big O."

The height of bodybuilding competition and a beauty pageant of sorts, the contest takes place over a weekend in Chicago, pumping up with a press conference. That's where I got my first glimpse of the "talent" wearing clothes. Many had 55-inch chests, 24-inch biceps, and 32-inch thighs. The average statistic was 250 pounds, with 3 percent body fat. One guy (5 foot 9, 260 pounds) who was dressed in a white linen jacket and baggy pants to accommodate his gigantic quads, reminded me of a refrigerator. "Here, there is no such thing as being too big," said a man sitting next to me. The only thing small about these guys were their posing trunks and shrunken scrotums from excessive steroid use.

First, the promoters made an announcement that the athletes would be tested for "all illegal drugs" and told everyone that anyone using them would be disqualified after the competition. (From the looks of the mega-huge contestants, there wouldn't be any contestants left.) That's when I got a good look at the female bodybuilders vying for the Ms. Olympia contest. (Average stats: 160 pounds with 5 percent body fat.) The male testosterone they were taking had transformed these chicks into square-jawed Amazonians who looked like Patrick Swayze in drag. As they answered questions with manly voices, I glanced at my *Muscle & Fitness* magazine, which listed the side effects of testosterone on women ("masculination from androgenics effects of anabolic steroids include facial hair, male pattern baldness, and clitoral enlargement"). Questions I was dying to ask the girls included "How often do you shave?" "Is that a toupee you're wearing?" and "Do you have to strap it down before you put on a bathing suit?"

After the press conference, one of the competitors tried to pick me up by sending over his trainer to introduce us. After we were introduced, he told me I was stylin'. (It worked.) A few minutes later, after his trainer "painted" him with tanning lotion for that orangy "fake bake" look, we all hung out in their room and had lunch. I had a muscle-building snack (a Steel Bar) while he ate a hunk of salmon steak and white rice washed down with protein supplements, multivitamins, carnitine (increases exercise endurance), creatine (increases muscle size and strength), HMB (stimulates muscle growth), vanadyl sulfate (makes muscles bigger), chromium (metabolises fat), and herbal diuretics (reduces water retention). For dessert, we went into the bathroom, where I watched "Big Boy" lift his skimpy briefs and shoot up testosterone in his butt, the same place where he also shoots insulin and HGH (human growth hormone). As far as drug testing was concerned, Mr. Olympia is not exactly the Olympics. I stared at his track-marked butt, which looked like a human pin cushion, and thought "All of this just to look good." And I thought I was vain for getting makeovers and mud masks at Bloomingdale's.

After lunch and 'roids, we talked about bodybuilding and girls. Both the trainer (who was also huge) and Big Boy told me they originally started lifting weights to "get chicks."

"But now," said the trainer, "when the two of us go out, average chicks are intimidated by our size."

"They think we are freaks," said Big Boy. Then I asked if he ever had sex with a Ms. Olympia contestant, and Boy recounted the story: "I went down there and it was way too muscular, you know, the whole area, and when I saw her enlarged clitoris, I had to run out of the room. It looked like a cross between a baby penis and a doggy dick." Pretty.

This story obviously brought back fond memories for the trainer, who said, "My last girlfriend was great. She loved the fact that when I am cycling (on testosterone), I can have five or six orgasms a day without losing my erection. On testosterone I have a hard-on twenty-four hours a day." He added, "Today we had to leave the hotel room to take turns masturbating." When I asked Big Boy if it was true that testosterone shrinks the testes, he said it does, but it makes his penis grow "anywhere from a half inch to three-quarters of an inch." This news combined with the thought of a perpetual boner persuaded me to say "yes" to his offer of being his date for the banquet following the finals on Saturday night.

Before I left, he let me give him a "power hug." I grabbed his massive latissimus dorsi and killer abdominous rectus, then rubbed my hands over his pharmaceutical-grade pectorals. His body felt like a hunk of sculpted rock covered with skin. I have never felt such a man. Then I "accidentally" brushed against his barbell. It felt like a Steel Bar. Suddenly, my clitoris erectus felt like it was on steroids.

The next day, I went to the convention center to check out the Expo and mingle with the muscle-junkie/bodybuilding crowd. Predominately male, the room was packed with pumped-up guys who were either personal trainers, bodyguards, or bouncers or just looked like them. A lot of men were showing off their muscles and wearing tight T-shirts with slogans like SHUT UP AND PUMP, HAMMER STRENGTH, GET HUGE, and GET FREAKY. One guy was wearing a HOOTERS T-shirt. (This is about as effective for picking up girls as wearing one that says, I'M WITH STUPID.)

I had landed on Planet Testes. But I enjoyed the high testosterone level—it was so masculine. (I have no problem being in a room with hundreds of horny men.) But aren't guys horny enough without added testosterone? A couple of guys suffering from the hyperactive side effects of steroids spotted some of the sexy "Fitness Olympia" girls (less built up than the

Ms. Olympias) and looked like they were pacing and pawing the ground, like racehorses being turned out for stud. At the EAS booth ("Better Bodies Through Chemistry") five buff babes with big boobs were standing in front of blenders mixing up protein/creatine drinks. Although the other five aisles were clear, there was a constant crowd in front of that booth. One girl's implants were so big, she struggled to keep them from dipping into the blender.

The men weren't the only ones in the convention hall who had big breasts. One guy told me he wanted to get breast reduction surgery for his "gynomastia" or testosterone-induced breast tissue growth—affectionately known as "bitch tits." ("Son, your mother and I think it's time you get a training bra.") Another guy told me, as he chewed on a Muscle Bar, "Yep, I've had pec implants and now I'm saving up for calves."

As I walked by the posing trunk booth, the wife-beater muscle T-shirt booth, and the hair transplant booth, I met a guy who told me he came to the convention in hopes of becoming a "spokesmodel" for Designer Protein, a company sponsoring a before and after contest. Another, wearing Joey Buttafuoco pants and Loni Anderson hair, told me he was a gym owner who wanted to have his photo taken with the bodybuilding stars who were on hand selling autographed 8 × 10 glossies of themselves for ten dollars. One guy, Mr. Gorgeous, a former Mr. Universe/Mr. Yugoslavia who was sitting behind the Met Rx booth, gave me a photo for free. He was so handsome that as he signed it, I had to control myself from asking if I could take a free look at his Met Rx Bar.

That night was the final judging for Mr. Olympia (first prize was $50,000, second $35,000—and lucrative vitamin and "health food" endorsements). The fourteen contestants had spent a year training—dieting, weightlifting, and chemically engineering their muscles—to get to this moment. The hopped-up crowd was rowdy and yelling posing directions to the line-up of superconfident, supermasculine he-men. With the light shining on their well-oiled layers of striated, "tanned" meat, they looked like oven-roasted, honey-glazed hams. Not expecting such built-up men to be acrobatic, I was surprised when one guy's routine ended with a split. (He left a dick 'n' balls–shaped oily print on stage, which glistened under the spotlight.)

After the compulsory seven poses, it was time for the "pose-down," where the last six finalists tried to impress the judges and beat the current four-time Mr. Olympia, Dorian Yates. Lined up head to head, they sucked in their killer stomachs, puffed out their humongous chests, and lifted up their massive arms. To impress the judges, they tried to push each other out of the spotlight, sticking their bionic biceps in front of one another's faces as the crowd went wild. It was pure machismo as each of the strongmen fought for dominance. When the finalists were announced and Yates won for the fifth time, one of the contestants looked like he was going to kill someone. Another looked like a little boy who was ready to cry. As they handed out the muscleman trophy, the crowd booed and yelled, "The contest is fixed!" Caught up in the muscle mania, I yelled, "Go, Big Boy!" and "Shake your money maker!"

I never did make it to the banquet with my date, because he lost and had a 'roid rage (a temper tantrum when someone is "cycling" on steroids). Since I wasn't exactly cruisin' for a bruisin', I found my own muscle fest. Two bodybuilding couples I met that day invited me to a party in their suite, especially after I started asking them about their sex lives. Once I got there the hormones had already kicked in. They told me they were into "sensual wrestling encounters" and "nude matches." Their group of about twenty people looked like they were carbo-loading every substance known to man—their version of "drug testing." The lights were dim, the porno tape was playing, and one shirtless Mr. and Ms. Olympia wannabe couple was rubbing each other's implants with posing oil. Another attractive couple stripped then wrestled each other to the floor as he twisted her nipples. "Let's get physical" would be putting it mildly. One chick who looked like she had been on *American Gladiators* told me she made extra money from making "boob bashing" and "bare-breasted catfighting and face-sitting" videos.

For this crowd, foreplay was rough and the three half-naked couples on the floor looked like a high school wrestling match gone haywire—pinning, light punching, arm twisting, even hair pulling. "It's a release," explained one girl, who looked strong enough to punch out any guy. (Her rock-hard breast implants alone looked big enough for a knock-out.) "It's sort of a ritual with us," she told me. "It's a test of strength. My boyfriend likes that I'm really strong and finds it challenging. Wrestling each other is our foreplay." I admit, it was a turn-on in a caveman sort of way—especially when I heard the loud grunts of one guy who was pinning a girl down and it sounded like he was benchpressing 250 at the gym. Then I watched as the one of the wrestler couples went into the bedroom and left the door open. (He was getting "muscle head.")

After I watched them have a powerhouse orgasm, the guy came out of the bedroom and asked if I wanted to join in for a good "work out." (He was like the trainer guy who was capable of five to six orgasms.) Although this guy had an incredibly hard (to believe) body, I was definitely tempted to "pull his muscle." But I passed. Call me old-fashioned, but I didn't want to be the twentieth rep in his third set.

ANKA
ANONYMOUS

Checking into Sex Rehab

"My name is Anka and I am a sexaholic." This is how I introduced myself to a bunch of strangers at my first Sexaholics Anonymous meeting in the basement of a New York City Catholic church. I ended up here after a guy I met told me he was a "recovering sex addict." I thought he was kidding until he encouraged me to go to a meeting. Apparently, he seemed to think I had symptoms of sex addiction (it takes one to know one). But it did make me wonder, am I a sex addict or am I just horny? What's the difference? I really started to wonder when I said yes to a number of symptoms listed in the sexaholic's questionnaire: (1) Do you often think about sex? (2) Do you enjoy sexual humor? (3) Do you have a job somehow related to sex? and (4) Do you frequently masturbate?

Once I suspected that I could be a sex addict, I was off to

a meeting. All of the sexual addiction programs—Sexaholics Anonymous, Sex Addicts Anonymous (having a less strict definition of "sexual sobriety"), Sexual Compulsives Anonymous (predominantly gay), and Sex and Love Addicts Anonymous (focusing on love addiction)—are based on the twelve-step program developed by Alcoholics Anonymous. The only difference between an AA meeting and an SA meeting is that at a Sexaholics Anonymous meeting, instead of a coffee machine at the back of the room, they have a table filled with tubes of penis-desensitizing cream.

At my first meeting, I was surrounded by almost forty men—I was the only woman—who ranged in age from twenties to fifties. The purpose of these meetings is to break the cycle of sexually compulsive behavior by discussing it with others who also like sex a little too much. The "share" is a four-minute talk (or a fifteen-minute "long share") where each person reveals a personal history of his or her compulsion, how they are trying to "kick the habit," and (my favorite part) how they "act out" their sexual addiction. One guy couldn't stop buying lap dances, a second reported masturbation marathons, and a third was addicted to hanging around ladies' rooms because he got turned on to the sound of women urinating (tinkle addict).

Since a sex addict's sexual encounters may involve anonymous sex, one of the tools the programs use to help people recover is dating. Instead of having impersonal experiences, the idea is to humanize the other person and try to have some feelings for them other than just lust. I kept that in mind; from now on I will try to become friends with a guy before I use him for his penis.

At my first Sex Addicts Anonymous meeting, the men all talked about their overpowering desire for a high as if they were heroin addicts. They talked of "the quick fix," of "binge-ing," of "bottoming out." The cycle starts with fantasizing, having some form of sex, then feeling either guilty, humiliated, or just depressed afterward. The addict has sex again and again to make himself feel better. Then he literally gets strung out on orgasms (orgasm addict).

Masturbation is a big component of sexual addiction. One guy said he was so out of control that he had to take care of himself ten to twelve times a day. He said he masturbated so much that he lost his job because of it. ("Boss, I can't come into the office today because I sprained my wrist.") On his unemployment form he filled in "Reason for dismissal" with "Hand-job-related illness."

Like AA meetings, people announce their "anniversaries" and the group applauds. Then people are encouraged to meet afterward in a café for nonsexual "fellowship." (Since a couple of the addicts were hotties, I had my own definition of fellow-ship.) At the end of each meeting, everyone stands in a circle and holds hands for the serenity prayer and pep cheer. ("Keep coming back: it works when you work it!") At this point, I wished I'd worn gloves, considering I knew exactly where some of those hands had been before the meeting.

To hear more stories of uncontrollable sex, I went to a sexaholics meeting where many of the men explained that dis-closing their secrets helped them overcome their obsessive-compulsive behavior. Two of the men were Hasidic Jews and said that if the members of their orthodox religion knew they were in a sex addicts program, they would be thrown out of their community. One of them (who was married) told us about his obsession with a dominatrix who beat him with coat hangers. (His family was in the coat hanger business.) Another talked about his phone-sex problem, which was costing him hundreds a month. He became obsessed with one operator for three months, then made plans to meet her, at the risk of jeopardizing his marriage. When they finally met, he recalled, she weighed four hundred pounds. Everyone in the group laughed. Even the other sex addicts thought that was a good one.

These people needed to tell their stories; it was therapeutic. But sometimes I found their tales of sexual excess almost slapstick. The guy sitting next to me said he was addicted to going to the gym, sitting on the bike machine, watching girls in front of him on the StairMaster, and coming in his pants. He explained that every time he pedaled, his penis would rhythmically hit the side of the seat. (Thanks for sharing.)

At one meeting, the theme was "relationships" and how the sexual addiction affected them. One guy told the group that he had recently made his girlfriend pregnant, they were getting married soon, and he wanted desperately to curb his sexual appetite. He said he had had sex with hundreds of women a year, that after a while they became nameless, faceless, that he never felt satisfied and always wanted more. After he had had sex with every woman he knew, he progressed to strip clubs, where he spent four hours a night, along with all of his money. After a while, he couldn't separate fantasy from reality and began paying strippers to go home with him. He hit rock bottom when he found himself obsessively going to peep shows. One night he ended up uncontrollably masturbating in a dark booth even after he ran out of money, and the peep show security pounded on the door and threw him out on the street. Another guy told us how he loves his wife but can't seem to control his sexual behavior. "I have sweet sex with my wife," he said, "which is great, but then I go and have the kind of sex I *really* like." Then he confessed the incredible guilt he felt when he returned home to his sweet wife right after he went to a gay sex club and had anonymous sex with three guys. (When he got back to his house, he opened the front door and yelled, "Honey, I'm homo!")

After everyone confessed their obsessions, I was asked if I wanted to share. I told everyone I was addicted to computer chat lines (especially the "wildsex" line). The next night, at a Sexual Compulsives Anonymous meeting, I told a bunch of gay men that I was addicted to pizza delivery boys. After I said that, I set off one guy who followed with stories of compulsively ordering flower delivery boys, UPS men, Con Ed guys, cable guys, etc. "I had days where I would call up repairmen all day even if nothing was broken," he confessed.

Listening to these stories of excess was like listening to a bunch of people at a Weight Watchers meeting talk about how they ate ten Big Macs, a dozen eggs, three bags of Doritos, and five pounds of bacon for lunch. But I couldn't help but feel compassion for these people, who were using sex to comfort themselves from life's disappointments. I like the sex addicts; many were intelligent and sensitive, not to mention sexy. So they have problems controlling themselves. I like highly sexual people; a man who can have ten orgasms a day is my kind of guy.

In fact, at every meeting I went to, there was always one guy I got the big-time hornies for. I admit that listening to a gorgeous man with intense sexual magnetism and an insatiable appetite tell how he masturbates in the car while he's driving kind of did something for me. He said his high was charming women, but after the sexual encounter he felt nothing. To feel something, he had to have more sex. As he told his story, I had a fantasy about how I could cure his addiction with my nymphomania.

At the meeting, I ran into a friend of mine, who told me during the break that he was having a fantasy about the guy sitting next to me. Meanwhile, that guy looked as if he was fantasizing about me. As we all fantasized about doing each other, I remembered the brochure that said "sex between people new to the fellowship and other members is discouraged." This is when I wondered what a good pickup line would be ("Do you come often?") and how I would introduce him to my friends ("So how'd you two meet?" "Oh, at a Sexaholics meeting. He was a compulsive masturbator and I was a compulsive fellator.").

So how does a man know if he's a sex addict? This is how you tell: If you pork someone three times, then you go to a strip club afterward, then you go home and beat the manmeat three more times, then call a phone-sex line but feel unsatisfied or depressed afterward, you could be a sex addict. If, however, you do all those things and feel great afterward, you're just really, really horny.

For women, it's harder to figure out. Especially because so few of the sex addicts were women. One of the guys suggested I go to either a Love and Sex Addicts Anonymous group or a Sexual Compulsives Anonymous meeting at the Lesbian and Gay Community Services Center. At both, I wondered if I would hear some tales of nymphomania, but discovered that I had joined gatherings of romantic obsessives—the trendiest recovery group of the nineties. ROs—mostly straight and gay women and gay men—get hooked on romantic fantasies more than sexual ones and find themselves obsessively fixating on someone who is completely unavailable. (One straight woman was obsessed with a married man; one gay guy went after the "most heterosexual, homophobic" man he could find.) ROs act out sexually to experience the romance they crave. The high is the initial infatuation period, the intoxication of the falling-in-love phase. I've heard women say that the one time they don't want to have sex is when they're upset about something else. They prefer comforting themselves by going shopping or eating a dozen Dunkin' Donuts. Men, on the other hand, use sex for stress management. If women acted out their problems as sexually as men did, there would be a lot more female flashers.

As I continued to go to more meetings, I found myself getting addicted to them. I realized, though, that I am not, in fact, a sexaholic. Sexaholics often feel unsatisfied after sex. Not me, I'm always Happy Girl afterward, unless, of course, I have selfishly been denied my satisfaction—then I'm a cranky bitch.

I also realized that I am not getting nearly *enough* sex, especially compared to the other people I met. Therefore, I have decided to up my masturbation to three or four times a day and start having more sex with more people—especially those I can't stand. I also plan on exposing myself in public, hiring naked guys to clean my apartment, and trying to hit on guys in men's bathrooms. And if I ever can't control the urge to tell any of these bedtime stories, I know exactly where to go.

Looking for
MR. RELIGIOUS RIGHT

Jesus Freakin' Dating

for some people, sex is better when it's dirty. Where there's shame there's excitement. And where there's religious dogma there's often shame. Since I was taught that sex is neither shameful nor sinful, I wondered what it would be like to go out with someone who thought it was. Would someone sexually repressed by religion go wild once they finally let loose? If so, where do I meet such a guy?

Hoping to find a Jesus freakin' Bible Beltin' man, I went down to Washington, D.C., for the Washington for Jesus rally on the Capitol lawn. "Isn't God the greatest?" shouted the preacher to a crowd of thousands. "If you want Jesus Christ to set you free, just wave at me!" As everyone did the wave, he screamed, "Generation X stands for ex-homosexuals!

Ex-fornicators!" Then the choir belted out a song about how Jesus loves everybody.

While standing in line to buy an Oral Roberts University T-shirt ("Class of 69"), I met a twenty-eight-year-old graphic designer who lived in Brooklyn who was with his fellow church members. After we talked for a while, he invited me to attend his Bible study group in New York. Then we walked back to the lawn to witness the "miracle" healing service given by televangelist Benny Hinn. "This woman has painful kidney stones!" he yelled into the microphone, waving his hands over her head. "And this woman has thyroid fibroids!" After they were "healed," they all looked so relieved that I was tempted to go up and see if he could do something about my godforsaken hemorrhoids.

After I got back to New York, I pursued my Christian dating with the guy I met in Washington. On the second date, I tried to kiss him, but he wouldn't let me. On our third date, he kissed me but backed off when he started getting excited. He said he was very attracted to me but he was a "believer." And he didn't believe in premarital sex. I said okay, but on the fourth date I told him to "just pretend we're married" and we started to make out. He even did the "laying of hands" on my "church bells," but pushed me away when he started to get the feeling of a higher power rising from his Bible Belt. The fifth time we got together, he told me we should "break up" because I was pressuring him into sex. I tried to convince him to "put out for Jesus," but he wouldn't. (It probably didn't help that I asked, "Whaddaya frigid?")

One Sunday morning while watching the *700 Club*, I saw

an ad for the Christian Dating Service—"for those interested in quality relationships." I decided to send away for the confidential membership application. The top of it read: "The word of God exhorts us not to deceive one another as brethren in Christ." After I filled out the basics like name, address, and occupation (I put "social worker"), they asked, "How does Jesus Christ relate to your life?" I thought it would be good to say, "I let Jesus Christ make all my decisions." Then, Jesus made me enclose a photo and write out a check for $299. I answered the rest of the questions. Under "List two hobbies that you enjoy," I wrote "furniture restoration" and "cooking" instead of what I really wanted to put: "bongmaking" and "dildo carving." Under "What sports do you enjoy?" I put "swimming" and "bicycling" instead of "foxy boxing," "mud wrestling," and "vaginal Ping-Pong."

The man from the Christian Dating Service called to tell me he gave my number to a member. "You'll like 'im," he said. "You two will have a lot in common. And he's very high-profile. Happy dating!" I reviewed the dating service's "How-to for ladies" flyer. It said, "Keep in mind that it is 'ministry' to sit down to tea or coffee or dinner. You've touched someone's life in doing this."

My first "ministry" was with Jeff, a thirty-two-year-old self-described "clean-cut" guy from New Jersey who said he was hoping to find a "clean-cut girl." To my surprise he was good-looking, with dark hair and nice brown eyes. He was a personnel manager who said he'd interviewed thousands of people. After interviewing me, he said he was looking for someone who leads a religious life, someone who is "virtuous," someone who is "virginal," someone who likes children. (Wanted: breeder stock.) When a Pamela Anderson–like babe walked by our table, I asked him, "So what do you think of women who dress sexy?" "Women who dress in tight shirts and short skirts are asking for it," he said as I looked down at the short and tight outfit I was wearing. He seemed disappointed by me, as though I didn't meet his "high moral standards." In fact, he was looking at me as if I were the daughter of Satan. He looked especially horrified when I accidentally used the Lord's name in vain and blurted out, *"Jesus H. Christ! Where's our goddamn coffee?"*

Like the other guys from the service, this one was seriously looking for a wife. (At least he wasn't afraid of a relationship; most of the guys I've gone out with thought that giving me an orgasm was too much of a commitment.) Yet he told me he "believed in the Bible one hundred percent" and would never have sex with a woman again unless she was his wife. Otherwise, he said, sex would be degrading. (Isn't that when it gets good?)

Since the Christian Dating Service offered the possibility of either marriage or celibacy, I looked elsewhere. Hoping to find someone a little more rock 'n' roll, I flew to Dallas for a Christian rock concert, a two-day event featuring eleven bands, designed to "draw a crowd of youth who will be able to grow in Christ." On the way over, I drove past a bunch of big ol' churches the size of Kmarts with neon signs. Once I got there, the Metroplex Covenant Church was already packed with guys with sideburns and the occasional dimple piercing, cropped blue hair, and matching blue T-shirts, guys and girls with dyed-black hair and white skin, and ska boys with Vegas lounge suits. My chances for meeting new Christian friends were looking good. Since everyone was friendly, I started asking people about sex. One twenty-two-year-old girl who was cultivating a hard-core Goth look told me she was a "neo-virgin" since she was born-again two years ago. ("My hymen grew back! It's a miracle!")

Although some had recently been born-again, most of the four hundred people there were second- and third-generation Christian fundamentalists whose parents taught them that sex was wrong and embarrassed them into a "Don't even think about doing it" mind-set. One nineteen-year-old virgin told me his father "embarrassed and humiliated" him after catching him with a triple-X porno movie, telling him he would "burn in hell" if he kept watching them. After him, I talked to a group of guys who turned out to be thirteen and fourteen. (I like younger men, but I draw the line at thirteen year-olds with pimples and braces.)

When a Green Day/Rancid–clone neo-punk band played, a bunch of boys started "skanking," a dance that looked like a cross between moshing and a conga line. The music and fashion statements were being used to encourage young Christians to embrace the lifestyle; the music sounded anarchistic but the lyrics were about Jesus. The audience seemed to accept it with *Stepford Wives* compliance.

If anyone would be getting any sex, I thought, it would be the guys in the bands. So I tried hitting on the guys in one of the hard-core bands. One was a twenty-seven-year-old virgin. Another was twenty-four and married, and a third had a girlfriend of three years whom he had only kissed. When I asked the two single guys how they avoided temptation, they both answered, "Cold showers." What do you get when you take the drugs *and* the sex out of rock 'n' roll? Blue hair and blue balls.

Watching the bands and the boys, I couldn't help but wonder where all the testosterone went. I asked one eighteen-year-old with a green Mohawk if he ever masturbated. "The Bible teaches that masturbation is sex, and sex is a sin," he told me. (Dictionary definition of *oxymoron*: "teenage boys who *don't* masturbate.")

One guy told me he was saved just a week ago. He thought that surrendering to Jesus would help control his urges. He told me he had been "going to the most decadent places that put him in sexual situations." "Like where?" I asked. That was the first place I wanted to go.

At Bar One, I fell into the depths of instant lust at the sight of a sweet 'n' tall boy with dyed-black Nick Cave hair and piercing green eyes. We flirted and he asked me to sit in a booth with him. He was a Capricorn. His turn-off was country-western gospel. His turn-on was my fishnet stockings, which he couldn't seem to take his hands off. He was hot. He was also, it turned out, the son of a preacher man. He believed that organized religion was about trying to "change people's beliefs" and preferred a more "molecular," "circular" approach to spirituality. In fact, he enjoyed sinning. When I felt his heavenly buns, I was filled with impure thoughts. But we didn't have sex because we were saving ourselves until we got married.

The next day, Sunday, "the Lord's day," I invited him

over to my hotel room for some "Bible studies." I tempted him. He had "the body of Christ" (I Corinthians 12:12–27). His penis was resurrected and he worshipped at the altar of my Wonderbra. Then we sinned. He yelled, "Hallelujah!" He filled my holiness. Praise the Lord! I prayed for the Second Coming. Amen.

OOOHS and

John Minh Nguyen

►ΔααHHʃ

PLEASE

COME AGAIN!

Contemplating the Big O

Orgasms: For some people they're sinful; for others they're mystical. The word originates from the Greek *orgasmos*, "to swell up," and translates from Indian as "to climb the ladder." The French discreetly refer to it as "the sneeze in the loins," or see them as *la petit mort*. Although most people have them, I rarely hear anybody talking about them. I never see people at cocktail parties wearing buttons that say ASK ME ABOUT MY ORGASMS.

I remember my first orgasms vividly. I was six and jumping up and down on a mattress at a furniture store. As the corner of the mattress rubbed me in the right place, I went into spasms. Just at that moment, a big, manly salesclerk lifted me up, spun me above his head, and yelled, "Airplane!" I had no idea what the hell was going on, but it does explain why I find myself developing crushes on pilots and mattress salesmen.

My second orgasmic surprise was just as dramatic but more traumatic. When I was nine, our poodle Mack stood on his hind legs and grabbed my thigh. Then he humped my leg and ejaculated all over it. I was the only nine-year-old in the neighborhood who was sexually molested by the family dog. (After that, we took him to obedience school and enrolled him in a sex-offender program.)

Unfortunately, my mishaps with the male orgasm would repeat themselves in my future sex life with humans. When I was sixteen, I made out with a guy in a parking lot at the school dance. My date asked me to fondle his woodrow, which I did, but about a minute later, he had an "accident" on the front of my new skirt. While he went back inside and danced with other girls, I spent the next hour in the bathroom holding my skirt in front of the blow-dryer.

If there's one thing men know how to do, it's have an orgasm. Women see having one with a man as not only a physical bonding process but occasionally an emotional one as well. (That is, if we can stand the guy afterward.) Men, on the other hand, view it as a physical workout, culminating in the release of the he-man wad. Guys have a tendency to overestimate the appeal of their ejaculate. Whereas men think of it as "nectar of the gods," women consider it a smelly, glandular secretion that we have to wash off.

The problem with men and women is timing. While women are trying to have an orgasm, men are trying not to. To help my man avoid the dreaded premature ejaculation (or "dishonorable discharge"), I once tried the scrotal pull, a technique that requires tugging the manly jewels at their base to delay the orgasm. It worked, but for a week he sounded like a member of the Vienna Boys Choir.

One friend of mine swears she can "female ejaculate." I didn't believe her until she showed me an instructional video called *How to Female Ejaculate,* where a bunch of women sit around and masturbate together with gigantic vibrators and take turns ejaculating as the "jet-cam" zooms in.

Apparently, a small percentage of women can do this, the result of stimulating the urethral sponge (the G-spot), which causes the paraurethral gland to expel fluid. My friend discovered this while her boyfriend was performing oral sex and she squirted him in the eye. The next time he went down on her, he wore a pair of safety goggles.

I stuck with the Kegel exercises, which strengthen the pubococcygeul (the muscle that stops the flow of urine). This intensifies orgasms for both men and women by causing stronger contractions, in addition to tightening the equipment. After six weeks of doing Kegels while in the subway and waiting in line at the bank, I noticed that I was not only having stronger orgasms, but I could also remove the lug nuts from the wheels of my car.

When it comes to orgasms, there is no such thing as a bad one. While some are better than others, all are better than okay. There are many types, including the fusion orgasm, where two or more erogenous zones (e.g., the nipples and the prostate) are simultaneously stimulated, and the ESO (extended sexual orgasm), where the man learns to partially retain his juice during ejaculation through controlled breathing and tensing the pubococcygeul, resulting in longer male orgasms. Other varieties of climax include the slacker orgasm ("I'll just lie here while you do all the work"), the margarita orgasm ("I think I climaxed but I can't remember"), and the cin-o-rama, also known as the multiple orgasm.

There is also something called the altered-state orgasm, which occurs when the brain is flooded with serotonin, the feel-good neurotransmitter. Comparable to near-death and out-of-body experiences, altered states can be entered by different methods. Timothy Leary once said, "In a carefully prepared, loving LSD session, a woman can have several hundred orgasms." I don't know if I believe that, but I do know that I once did mushrooms in Finland and wanted to cop a few O's, but I could not locate my genitalia.

Another way to experience an altered-state orgasm is through S&M: when the body is overstimulated by pain, the slightest touch to the privates can bring on an intense orgasm. (The problem here is trying to figure out if someone is having an orgasm or suffocating under their leather hood.)

It's easy to tell when a man is ready to blow: the eyes roll back, the nostrils flare, the teeth clench, and the tendons in the neck pop; sort of like Henry Rollins in concert. Some women undergo more subtle physical changes, such as a deepening in the color of the vaginal lips due to increased blood flow. You know she's coming when her labia turn purple like a mood ring.

Although it's exciting to watch someone climax, most people's faces do not look camera-ready at the big moment. Even though they are experiencing pure pleasure, it's the same look as giving birth, crying hysterically, getting a root canal, or straining on the john.

Although orgasms may look ugly, they sound fabulous. When I first moved to New York, I lived in an apartment surrounded on all four sides by women. One night I heard one of my neighbors going at it barnyard style. I heard assorted grunts, barks, and howls. (I like roaring and gnawing, but clucking and quacking really turn me off.)

As an orgasm approaches, people start talking dirty. In the heat of the moment, the things people say to get off may have nothing to do with feminism or male sensitivity: "Oh, Roger, your big rod is ripping me apart" or "Oh, Susie, I want your hot, juicy box."

Some things are left better unspoken—like the fantasy you were having about three other people as you were exploding.

After the big eruption comes the afterglow. This is the time women want to hear sweet nothings like "Run away with me forever, *caru miu!*" Instead, we hear stuff like "Boy, did I ever lose a big load!" "I totally blew my nuts!" or "That was so much better than my hand!" (I'm actually competing with a guy's hand?)

While men are imagining physical images of many women, we are having our own scenario-driven fantasies leading up to the climactic peak. I fantasize about posing on the cover of a romance novel with Fabio: he seduces me in Italian, metaphorically lubing me up to a crescendo, playing me like a mouth orgasm. In our ecstasy, we knock over lamps and accidentally punch our fists through the drywall. As we reach our earth-shattering multiple orgasms, I yell, "Oh, my God, I'm coming!" And he screams out, "I can't believe it's not butter!"

talk FLIRTY to Me

Hair Tossing and Winking

I'm walking down the street and I see Johnny Perfect. Our eyes meet. My heart pounds. My womanhood swells. Our mating dance begins. Stud boy walks closer. I pucker my lips. He smiles. I smile back. Our flirtatious glances reach a crescendo as he approaches. He leans over and with a quivering voice whispers in my ear, "Can I see your nipples?"

Apparently, I brought out the animal in him. If I'd stood there any longer, he would have asked if he could sniff my butt.

In the jungle, sexual display is the first step in an elaborate ritual of mating. Chimp chicks flirt by conspicuously presenting their bright red rumps to the male chimpanzees. The males' response is to sit with their legs apart, showing off their monkey balls for the ladies. On the New York City subway, I often observe this same ritual—guys "adjusting" their crotches in response to attractive female passengers.

Among humans, flirting is the most artful form of social intercourse. It starts with a look, then a smile, and hopefully escalates into sparkling repartee. If a man says witty things to a woman, she may even think he is interested in her personality. When done well, it makes both parties feel desirable; when done badly, it makes a woman feel leered at. If done *really* well, women get goose pimples and men get boners.

"Love comes in at the eye," wrote Yeats. Eye contact is the essential starting point of flirtation. In the subway recently, I made intense eye contact with a guy sitting across from me. It was stimulating to exchange goo-goo eyes and smile back and forth as the train got more crowded. But both of us were afraid to make the first move. As he got up and left the train, I was reminded that eye contact doesn't lead to anything unless you seize the moment. At that point a total sleazeball got on the train. He didn't make eye contact with me, but he did seize the moment: as the train pulled into the station, he rubbed his erection against my leg like a dog. This is *not* considered flirting.

Flirting is mental foreplay; it's safe pre-sex. It can go on indefinitely, even with people you have no intention of sleeping with. It's harmless—depending on how far you take it or how married you are. And it can occur anywhere: at the beach, at a restaurant, at the gym (I always seem to attract men at the inner-thigh machine, when my legs are spread apart). Alternative settings include Moonie cult meetings (if it works out, you get a free wedding and a suit from Sears) and waiting in line to use the bathroom (this gives the two of you something in common to talk about—full bladders and expanding colons).

Flirting at a funeral is acceptable, but try to wait till the reception—don't expect a big response if you wink over the open casket. Going to a pro-choice rally is a good place for guys who want to appear evolved. There will be lots of chicks into premarital sex who will appreciate your interest in the women's movement. Refrain, however, from making placenta jokes.

Flirting styles vary according to geographical differences. In France, flirting seems more playful, more au naturel. You look at someone, they look at you, and the next thing you know you are sipping Château Margaux. Frenchmen know what women want (compliments) and know how to give them ("You intoxicate me"). The problem is that before they try to seduce you back to your hotel, they have to slip out and call their wives.

In Yugoslavia, the flirting is killer. In a Bosnian bar once, I heavily flirted with two masculine, square-jawed Balkan boys of steel. Meanwhile, the Croat and the Serb started arguing over me. All I could understand was the word *picka* (vagina). They were having a territorial dispute over who owned my demilitarized zone. As they broke out into a violent fistfight, I ran out of the bar in search of a helmet and a chastity belt.

In Italy, flirting is a national pastime. I was walking down the street in Milan and an Italian stallion winked at me from his car. I giggled, so he jumped out of his Alfa-Romeo, leaving it in the middle of a busy intersection, creating a huge traffic jam. He ran down the street after me yelling, *"Bellissima! Ti amo!"* (Beautiful! I love you!) *"Dònna!"* (You are a real woman!) He continued to chase me down the street as horns honked and people waved their fists in the air, swearing in Italian and yelling, *"Muovati, Romeo!"* (Move it, Romeo!) When I asked, "What about your car?" he said, "My Alfa will never be as important as you." These are the moments that women live for. (This explains why women like Fabio.)

Los Angeles is a great place to flirt. All you have to do is drive around in a convertible, wave at people, then tell them to pull over ("Park 'n' chat"). New York City, however, is the worst place to flirt. New Yorkers do not want to make eye contact with anyone. If they do, someone will ask them for money. If they look too vulnerable and cheery, someone will eventually mug them.

Since New Yorkers are too paranoid to walk down the street smiling, I had to develop guerrilla flirting tactics to overcome their defensiveness. For a week, I aggressively flirted everywhere I went. On the street, I smiled. At the grocery store, I winked. In the produce department, I bent over.

After a week of flirting I thought about techniques that worked on me (the guy on a motorcycle who drove by with a bouquet of flowers a few minutes after I smiled at him). And the ones that didn't (the guy who winked at me while holding hands with his wife).

Women like the sensitive, caring approach. If a sexy guy walked up to me in the feminine hygiene aisle of the drugstore, held up a box of sanitary napkins, and asked, "Have you tried maxi pads with wings?" I would think he was hot. It would show that he cared about my feminine protection.

As part of my week of deliberate flirting in New York City,

I experienced what most men do: rejection. One reason people don't flirt more often is the fear of being turned down. If you do decide to flirt with lots of people, you have to admit to yourself that some people will be majorly not into you. One day on the mean streets of New York, I looked at dozens of guys. Although many flirted with me, others looked the other way, some gave me dirty looks, a number looked at me like Charles Manson, and a few came on to the gay man I was with. But I forged on anyway. I decided to develop a tough skin and not let rejection shake my self-confidence. I went out on the road again, eyeing, smiling, winking, batting my eyelashes, shaking my booty, blowing kisses, and tossing my hair. After a bunch of rejections, I considered going home for some auto-erotic asphyxiation.

But once you learn to take rejection in stride, flirting becomes addictive. It's harmless, it's fun, and it can lead to sexual intercourse. So I did it again. I went to a family wedding, where my mother pointed out a six-foot-four side of beef. We made eye contact and I flirted with him shamelessly. As the ceremony proceeded, we continued to eyeball each other. At the reception, my aunt introduced us. Unfortunately, it turned out he was fifteen. It also turned out that he was my second cousin.

b e ƒ o r e P L A Y

First Dates

ƒrom exciting to nerve-racking, first dates are the time when two strangers subconsciously sniff each other while inputting selective data into their brains. While women are trying to figure out if we even like the guy, men are wondering if they will be getting laid. For women, first dates are when we investigate a man's family background, sexual history, and life goals. For men, first dates are when they visualize what we look like naked.

When women prepare for the first date, it's a major production. This is the time we try on ten outfits, then decide to wear something else. Meanwhile, men's preparation is searching for a shirt that doesn't stink.

In the last four decades, dating has gone through a schizoid metamorphosis. In the fifties courtship was taken seriously. A man brought a woman flowers and boxes of candy before he met her parents. Men were gentlemen and women were creatures to be courted and complimented. By the late sixties, a date had become two hits of acid and lots of free love. By the seventies, dating had become really uncool: Why bother going out on a date when you could go to an orgy? In the early eighties dating consisted of meeting someone at a club and having sex in the bathroom before going home. In the nineties, aversion to excess combined with the fear of waking up with gnarly venereal warts means keeping the first date as casual as possible. Which is why today a formal first date seems, well . . . dated.

Now, hanging out in groups is fashionable. When you're out with someone new and five other people, there is no pressure to act any different from how you would with your friends. And if you decide you can't take each other, making a quick exit is much easier. Recently, I was asked to hang out with an actor guy and his two buddies. My aspiring actor "date" seemed more interested in acting out Tropicana commercials ("You can't get a better juice") and Snickers commercials ("Snickers satisfies ya") with his buds than talking to me. Since the date provided no intimacy, the only thing I learned about the guy was that he had no future as an actor.

While Americans tend to hang out, Scandinavian daters have taken hanging out to a new extreme. A first date in Sweden consists of drinking a fifth of vodka and brooding.

By the time you're ready for the good-night kiss, it's a good idea for guys to look for signals indicating whether she wants you to go any further. If she shakes your hand and jumps out of the car, chances are she doesn't. (This didn't stop one of my dates from trying to kiss me through the window of a moving cab.) If she starts tonguing your tonsils, it's a good predictor that there could be possible penetration the next time out. Make sure you have finished eating before kissing, however. My last date tried to deep-throat me after eating a bag of potato chips, and I could taste the chunky drool of his Pringles.

And one more thing: heavy drinking and dating don't mix. My most recent drinking date started out with martinis at the Yale Club. After my charming date made amusing conversation, he showed me photos of his father and grandfather on the football team. Then he had more martinis. Afterward, we went to a party in someone's loft where he consumed two beers and uncounted shots of tequila. As the evening wore on, his behavior disintegrated. By the end of the night, he had eaten rice from the buffet with his bare hands, made out with another girl in the bedroom, and when introduced to my brother, said, "Eat my shorts." His finale was lying on his stomach on the dance floor, doing the swim in a pile of his own puke. These were signs the date was not going well.

You don't want to tell the person your last name.

You start having sexual fantasies about the person serving
you drinks.

You fall in love with the violinist who serenades your table.

You do everything in your power to suppress your personality.

Your date is flirting with every person in the room but you.

You wonder if your date knows anyone you could go
out with.

You order a double espresso to keep from falling asleep.

You seriously reconsider going on *Singled Out*.

Your date goes to the bathroom and never comes back.

You *don't* visualize what your date looks like with no
clothes on.

Your date never shows up.

ᴀ ɴ ᴋ ᴀ ' ꜱ SECRET

Lingerie Lover

Lately I've noticed that every time a guy comes over to my apartment while I'm getting ready, he's making himself at home with my Victoria's Secret catalog. Hypnotized by the merchandise, he studies it with the same attention he gives *Big Boobs* magazine. It seems the only time women get a man's undivided attention is when we are naked or half-naked in sexy underwear.

Of course, everybody likes something different. Some guys want us to look innocent while others want us to look like cheap hookers. And I'm sure there's a jogger-bra maniac out there standing behind a tree touching himself at every New York City Marathon.

Some men become so obsessed with lingerie that they get aroused by the specific object itself. Hello, fetish. They have names for these things. Kleptophilia is a fixation where people get turned on not only by the fetish item but by stealing it. Then there's mysophilia, where guys get turned on sniffing used panties. In Tokyo's porno district, for 3,000 yen (about $30), you can buy the soiled panties of teenage girls from vending machines. (I wonder what's written on the machine in Japanese: "Enjoy Coke and panty! Get a whiff of Pepsi generation!")

A few men, in fact, enjoy women's lingerie so much they start wearing it themselves. Usually men who like to wear the panties in the family are perceived as being gay, but not my dates. One guy I went out with peeled off my panty hose and insisted on wearing them before we had sex. (He was a control-top freak.) The second time we did it, he slipped into my panty hose again. When he put on my bra, I was afraid I would soon be dating Mrs. Doubtfire.

My own lingerie jones is bras. I like plunging my tatas into lace, satin, and vinyl, and I love shopping at Frederick's of Hollywood. That's where a grandmother in polyester selling butt pads and peekaboo bras once asked me my cup size. I could barely spit it out before she grabbed my left hooter and proclaimed, "You're a 36C."

Being a bra-aholic, I also love the Wonderbra, lingerie's biggest development. In the seventies women burned their bras; today they want a little postfeminist push-up action. The Wonderbra is a technological advancement, a bra scientifically designed to make real breasts look like fake ones. (One guy I know thinks this is false advertising, yet he's the first to admit he approves of implants.)

In addition to techno bras, I have also tried edible undies. The strawberry candy pants were exciting at first, and I liked having them licked, but when I started sweating, they started melting and stuck to my pubic hair. After a night of passion, I woke up with a sticky wedgie. This is when I peeled off my breakfast treat: Hairy Cracklin' Fruit Rollups. (New! Berry with dingles!)

While I'm out dropping $200 on bustiers and thong bodysuits, most guys are wearing the same $3 pair of crusty briefs they've had on all weekend. I'm waiting for the day when men feel the pressure to compete with bionic penis implants. That's when someone will invent the Wonderjock, to make the penis look longer, wider, and harder, while lifting and separating the scrotum.

When it comes to shopping for women's lingerie, some men are hoping to pick up something more than just under wear. On a recent visit to Victoria's Secret, I heard one of my eager male companions say to the other, "Let's take a walk-through and check out the chicks in the 36D section." If it were up to guys to design lingerie stores, they would install pool tables, have beer on tap, and hire live models who walk around and mingle with the customers in between dancing on poles.

Since most men aren't fluent in lingerie lingo and there's so much to choose from, men are even more confused about what women want. Often the things men choose reveal more about what *they* want. When I'm out shopping for lingerie, I always seem to notice a repressed-accountant type delicately fingering a black-widow corset, or a burly construction worker buying a tasteful silk nightgown. A male prostitute told me once that he gets really turned on by women who wear white, virginal lingerie.

A man needs to get an insight into a woman's personality before making a lingerie purchase, especially during the pre-porking phase of dating. (Once a guy I hardly knew bought me a white flannel nightgown and I was charmed, but when I tried it on, I looked like a cast member from *Hee Haw.*) The biggest problem occurs when a woman reacts to a man's tacky purchase (like a neon-orange lace French maid's uniform) with "You want me to wear *that*?" Our idea of looking sexy might be a million miles away from his fantasy, which consists of making us look as if we're posing for the cheesy photo on the side of a vibrator box.

The best solution for men is to go lingerie shopping with a girlfriend, but for those men who are contemplating going alone, I offer two suggestions. Size counts. First, when buying a bra for your honey, never say to the salesgirl who asks for her measurements, "They're about your size. How about if I stand behind you and feel yours?" Second, when buying crotchless underwear, don't ask, "What size do these things come in— small, medium, large, and two-car garage?"

oNe Night ONLY

Sex with a Stranger

It was a perfect night. A dreamy red-sand beach in Maui, a sexy surfer boy, and me. I waxed his board, he juiced my pineapple, and we both had volcanic eruptions with hot lava flow. The next morning, he caught a wave, I caught my flight, and we never saw each other again. I always wondered what happened to him. Four years later, I'm walking down the streets of New York, and I see him sitting cross-legged on the street, homeless and begging for money.

One-nighters are the first time you have sex with someone and the last. They're not exactly trendy, but they do happen. They can occur anytime and anywhere, but the opportunities particularly present themselves on vacation ("You're leaving *tomorrow?*"), overnight business trips ("Me, married? Oh, no, I'm single"), trips to Europe ("You don't speak *any* English?"), or during "fleet week" in New York City ("Hello, sailor.")

Sometimes you meet someone you have an instant animal attraction to, and the prospect of having cheap, thrilling sex with them *that* night is so intoxicating and overwhelming that you consciously decide to ignore five things about them (e.g., they dress tacky, they have an obnoxious personality) in favor of the one thing you like about them (their body). One side of your brain is telling you "no, don't" while the other side is telling you "Yes, do" (the "weenie brain" side). There is a point where you meet someone when you know the person is not right for you, the moment when you say to yourself, "This person is totally wrong for me—I have no rapport with them whatsoever. In fact, this person is a moron, but they are so gorgeous I'm going to have to sleep with them anyway."

First-night encounters are usually not the start of a beautiful, long-lasting relationship. Only on rare occasions do they lead to two-nighters or a "sex buddy" situation. This is because most people have one set of criteria for choosing a potential girlfriend or boyfriend ("someone fun to hang out with, someone with a similar taste sensibility who shares my interests, and someone I wouldn't be embarrassed to take home to my mother") and another set of criteria for one-nighter material ("I'm horny").

Heavy drinking is one reason people end up having one-nighters in the first place, but that doesn't mean that drinking ten tequilas then jumping into bed with a total stranger is such a good idea. How bad the person looks the next morning is in direct proportion to how many drinks you've consumed the night before. If you've had twelve shots and the person seemed like a nine, the next morning they could easily drop to a two. It is a horrifying moment when you wake up and realize you have fornicated with The Swamp Thing.

Once, after drinking way too many Smirnoffs, I brought a guy back to my bachelorette pad. Just as I was impressing him with my fellatio skills, my gag reflex was triggered and I puked on his dick. (It looked like creamed corn on the cob.) I cleaned it up with a handful of sawdust and a push broom. Needless to say, he never called me back for seconds.

Although alcohol and coke may facilitate a one-night encounter, other drugs may complicate the experience. There's the "Special K one-nighter" ("I'm in a K-hole and I can't get up, let alone find the hole") and the "crystal meth one-nighter" ("Could you slow down? I'm getting a rug burn on my penis"). Prozac, on the other hand, gets even manic-depressives in the mood for a one-nighter ("I'm feeling good right now, so before I commit suicide, let's do it!").

Given the spontaneity of the one-nighter, the unexpected happens. Once I ended up at a guy's apartment, and as we started to "get busy," two of his friends showed up out of the woodwork, took off their shirts, got into bed with us, and started pawing me. For a minute, I thought I was in a petting zoo. I kicked them out. After about ten minutes, when the two of us went back to kissing, I felt a second tongue between my legs. I looked down and saw his dog trying to have sex with me. (Come to think of it, the dog did a better job than the guy.) After the dog left, I was afraid that his pet gerbil would get loose.

One-night gigs, however, offer the opportunity for sexual experimentation. It is possible that you might try something you've always wanted to but were afraid to ask. It's also possible to find out that you like something you didn't know you did. One friend of mine, a former Vegas showboy, picked up a guy at a club, took him home, and the guy started face-slapping him. He liked it. Really liked it. Bitch-slapped the guy back. From there, they progressed to butt punching. After that, he added face slapping and butt punching to his repertoire. (He had to stop, however, when he missed and accidentally punched a guy in the nuts.)

The scary part of one-nighters (besides the obvious disease paranoia) is when you realize later how much you *didn't* know about the person you just slept with. (Once I forgot the guy's name the next morning and had to sneak a look in his wallet when he went to the bathroom.) What they tell you the morning after could be reason enough never to have a one-nighter again (like the guy who told me, "I have multiple-personality disorder," leading me to wonder which one of "him" I'd just slept with).

When I first moved to New York, innocent me slept with a handsome and smooth guy who called me the next day and said, "You know, I was going to steal your money, your jewelry, and your credit cards, but I decided not to because I thought you were so nice." After that I made sure that if I ever had another one-nighter, I would dust my breast for fingerprints.

Once the sex is over, the awkwardness of the one-night stand stares you in the face. This is the "should I stay or should

I go" phase of the evening. Some people look so anxious to leave you wonder if they have a cab waiting outside; others want to stick around, asking, "Can we do it again?" One line that often works on someone who doesn't get the hint is "If you don't leave right now I'm calling the police."

If you do spend the night together, as soon as you wake up is the time you have to reintroduce yourselves to each other, the time when you find out what you should have the night before (*"You just got out of prison yesterday?"*). This is the moment when two people who got naked together and performed intimate acts on each other's genitals don't even want to kiss good-bye and end up shaking hands. It's also when two people who have nothing to say to each other and have nothing in common say, "Call me sometime," and exchange phony phone numbers.

Although women probably have as many one nighters as men do, they don't seem to work as well for us. It has to do with two other reasons. Once a guy drops "the big load," his behavior changes. First, women find it alienating when a guy goes from a Casanova to "the cranky guy who coldly throws me out of his apartment before his girlfriend comes home." The even bigger reason for our dissatisfaction is that half the time sex happens so fast we don't even have an orgasm. If we do it immediately after we meet a guy, there may not be as much in it for us; we could get one minute of foreplay, a premature ejaculation, and an immediate getaway. (This is known as a quarter-nighter.)

SEXperiments

John Minh Nguyen

WANTED:

Able-bodied Men

Exciting Opportunities for Sexual Positions

at the Anka Institute of Human Sexuality, the goal is to further the boundaries of carnal knowledge. Like sexual researchers before me—Masters and Johnson, Alfred Kinsey, and Shere Hite—I will examine the various aspects of human desire and response. Through scientific experimentation, advances will be made, theories will be launched, and the quality of life will be improved. In the well-equipped Anka Love Lab, the sexual habits of the modern male will be studied, dissected, and probed. Among other throbbing questions, I will attempt to explain the physics of penile hydraulics.

To continue my explorations, I will need a staff, which includes a brilliant and unusually gifted research assistant, a boy laureate capable of performing complex tasks. As part of his duties, he will undergo a battery of physiological tests including endurance experiments and product reviews. My ideal research boy will have an insatiable curiosity and a fertile imagination. He will also look good in a lab coat and no pants.

To facilitate the process, I placed a help-wanted ad in *Details* that read, "Position open as Anka's research assistant, short-term assignment with generous employee benefits. You will be accommodated for a weekend of scientific inquiry and study in New York City. You will be a guinea pig, but you will love it. Various duties may include endurance testing and physical therapy. Send photo, résumé, and/or a brief letter stating your qualifications. Enthusiastic attitude a plus."

More than seven hundred strapping young bucks from all over the USA and Canada answered, eager to assist me in my sexology studies. Men of strength and endurance—bodybuilders, physical therapists, all-American football players, and marines responded to the call of duty. Also applying were homeless guys looking for a place to stay, guys who sell their own plasma, and slackers with no jobs who spend a lot of time "stimulating" themselves in their rooms at their parents' house.

Since I asked for credentials, few men hesitated to extol their virtues, like Bob, a software engineer, who said he was "ten inches soft." Another, who called himself Mr. Girth, promised that he would "make [my] vagina talk." Steve, a twenty-four-year-old from Washington, wrote, "I am an expert at cunnilingus and am proficient in G-spot massage." One guy put it succinctly and said, "I am very, very, very horny."

Since the research was of a scientific nature, I received many entries from medical students, doctors, and lab technicians. A med student from Ohio said he could administer CPR in case I went into shock, and an emergency medical physician from Michigan said he would take care of me if I "should sustain any injury during our research." This was good to know in case I OD'd on aphrodisiacs, passed out from multiple orgasms, or suffered a labial contusion.

For every qualified applicant, there was his unqualified counterpart, such as Bill from New Jersey, who listed among his credentials an "appearance on the *Richard Bey Show*. Topic: male sluts." His experience included "getting into a pushing match with Judd Nelson in a strip club on four tabs of mescaline." Another listed his special skill as being able to "produce an erection on command by simply contracting my sphincter muscle." A third listed his qualifications as "I masturbate a lot." In fact, several men listed this as their most impressive talent. Chris from Palo Alto said he saw me on *Rolanda* and confessed, "When you said on the show that you were having an orgasm right then and there, you were not alone."

For various reasons, I seem to be popular with the prison population. Paul, twenty-eight, in a California jail for the next three months on theft-related charges, describes himself as "superintellectual." (He has been an exotic dancer and his dream is to be in *Playgirl* magazine.) Zachary, incarcerated in Illinois in a sexual offender program, tells me he is trying to correct past "negative sexual behaviors" such as "masturbating in his palm and then shaking hands with women." He also confessed, "I would love to sniff your chair." Enclosed was a visitor information form.

One potential lab rat from Kansas got a head start on research by recounting his experiences with "sexual enhancement chemistry." Jon, who liked to experiment with testosterone and steroids, paid $5 in Mexico for a drug that "induces labor in women and other species." He went back to his hotel room, shot up a vial, and reported that "about ten minutes later my nipples began to tingle and my mammary glands began to swell, which lasted for about twenty minutes." With drugs like these, he could also get work as a wet nurse.

Will, a twenty-seven-year-old lawyer from Santa Monica, sent in a suggested reading list to help me with my research. These included a book on "acquired hermaphroditism," a photo book of animals defecating and urinating, and a children's book called *Everyone Poops.*

A couple of Romeos took the seductive approach to applying for the job. A twenty-five-year-old Colorado nature boy who called himself a "true craftsman" used woodworking as a metaphor for the proper way to treat a lady. "I start with the legs," he wrote, "then give the entire body of the piece a hand-rubbed finish." Joe from L.A. sent in an audiotape with Barry White in the background and him doing a voice-over because he'd been told he has a sexy voice. Bob from Arizona sent in front and side mug shots of his penis and wrote "research tool." Another guy sent in a photo of himself sitting on the toilet. Instead of sending *me* something, David from Oakland, California, asked if I could send *him* a pair of my used panties.

A few guys used the personal approach, like the guy who sent in a tape of himself having a "video dinner date" with me at the hunting lodge. Bob, from upstate New York, applied as a group. Sending in a photo of himself and his gang, he promised, "If selected, endurance testing won't be a problem."

Jason, a camp counselor, says his interests include "martial arts, supernatural research and science, religious philosophy, and discovering human potential." Describing his background, he wrote, "I first learned the potential to make pickups at work while selling shoes in the ninth grade. This is where I learned to fondle the feet of total strangers. At another job at Kmart, while patrolling the aisles and running the Blue Light Special, I would notice the wandering eyes of the apparel gals as they plotted our stockroom petting sessions." Jason's experience encouraged me to initiate a long-term study, *Sexual Activity in American Discount Stores*, with an adjunct study on retail perversion, emphasizing "agalmatophilia" (sexual arousal from store mannequins).

Equally as qualified was Dave, who describes himself as "an exotic island boy" whose hands-on experience includes a stint as a surfing instructor in Hawaii where he assisted females in "untangling their bikini bottoms." He now works at a Utah prison for troubled teens and has "learned to use restraints for those who do not obey orders." He notes, "I take the restraints home three times a week and practice. I am also currently a 'Glutemaster' salesman and have great buns."

After all the job applications were in, I narrowed the talent down to the ten most potent. My first telephone interview was with Rambeaux, a twenty-eight-year-old industrial/tribal vocalist/songwriter/Mental Landscape band member/emergency-room MD from Detroit who "has numerous contacts throughout the underground subculture, subgenius, and sub conscious." He also has "extensive knowledge of S&M and vampirism." He is tattooed, pierced, and recently had his arm branded. After he told me that branding "makes the skin raised," my first question was, "When the skin is sizzling, does it smell like chicken?" As he picked at it and took a whiff, he revealed that it actually smelled more like beef jerky.

My second applicant was another twenty-seven-year-old MD, a urology resident from New York City, who has a "technical knowledge of reproductive anatomy and the hands of a surgeon." He sounded so cute over the phone I wanted to pee my pants.

My other potential boy wonders included a twenty-five-year-old virgin and a forty-two-year-old virgin. Between both of these guys, I figured they would not only be open to anything but would have years' worth of sperm buildup that could result in a new speed record for premature ejaculations.

Whomever I choose, wherever we go, research boy and I will forge on. We will explore the boundaries of the sexual frontier. We will conquer the erotic unknown. Through teamwork and togetherness, we will discover better loving through chemistry. Science awaits us.

Research Boys Get to Work

in the Love Lab

Now that the Anka Institute of Human Sexuality has opened its doors, it will dedicate itself to the study of the male libido. Through stimulating lab work and penetrating field research, the institute will explore the boundaries of the horny frontier.

To facilitate these scientific sexplorations, research grants have made it possible to complete a variety of studies from pleasure-threshold analysis to the effects of various stimuli on erectile tissue. Although I enjoy initiating projects myself, I cannot accomplish certain experiments on my own because, well, I don't have a penis.

My boy wonder must be willing to experiment and be exploding with scientific inquiry. Ideally, Über Boy will be endowed with special skills—he will be able to climax three times a day and be capable of lifting heavy objects with his erect organ.

After reviewing five hundred applications, ten semifinalists emerged (the only ones left, considering so many of them were incarcerated). Since our work is of an intimate nature, it was essential to access sexual chemistry, accomplished through an interview/date.

Head-hunting for research boys became research in itself. Some did not make it past the initial interview. One twenty-eight-year-old aspirant was so excited by the questions that he and the two friends he brought along sat and giggled like Beavis and Butt-head. Another slacker candidate wanted to have sex with the boss but didn't want to do any work. (It's hard to get good help these days.)

I quickly found out that despite their braggadocio about their own size and studliness, several candidates were unwilling to probe the unknown (this is known as scaredy-cat syndrome).

When faced with the pressure to put out, their previous claims of being sexual adventurers shrank, along with their research equipment. When they realized they would be sexually evaluated and physically scrutinized—an appraisal women are subjected to on a daily basis—they chickened out. (This is known as flaccid weenieism.)

My first applicant, research boy #1, was a twenty-six-year-old model wannabe who bragged that his debutante mother never dated anyone who hadn't gone to Yale or Harvard. I asked him to escort me to a Motown records company party. There he referred to several men as "guineas" and kept asking me if I'd "ever seen a black man naked." (Answer: yes.) Since he was so obnoxious, he became the perfect specimen for a behavioral experiment where the roles of men and women are reversed and the men are slaves. The next night we made a date to go to the Goddess Ball, a "celebration of dominant women." I figured he might look good in a dog collar and gag ball. Unfortunately, he stood me up. Needless to say, I had to fire him.

At the Goddess Ball, however, I did meet research boy #2, a twenty-five-year old gay TV producer. Seeking hands-on field data on the gay lifestyle, the next night we went to a leather bar. As I watched a cigar-smoking leather daddy cruise research boy, someone passed me an invitation to the bar's Butt Beautiful Night (I'm there). I asked research boy to help me relive the late seventies, when people did poppers in sex clubs. At the local all-male adult bookstore, we bought a vial sold under the name Liquid Incense. We inhaled a whiff, felt a momentary rush and a tingle. That's when he told me what poppers were used for (sphincter dilation). After I heard that, I was afraid to sit on the barstool.

Although I generally hired people I met in person, I did hire one research boy over the phone. A twenty-six-old doctoral student in clinical psychology, he will head the Chicago branch of the institute. His first project was comparison testing of vacuum-pump penis enlargers. In laboratory tests, the Overdrive, which guarantees to "blast you over the finish line," outperformed the Blue Veiner, although the latter was endorsed by the AAPP (American Association of Professional Pumpers). According to research boy #3's finding, "My penis didn't get any bigger, but my foreskin got three inches longer."

Research boy #4's desire to spread the seed made him the ideal candidate for work in the institute's "fertility research program." Our work began in the sperm bank. We were told that the donor must be under thirty-five, have two years of college, and provide extensive health and genetic background information. Once he was accepted, his love juice would be checked for "potency, consistency, high sperm count, and freezability."

I hoped that RB was virile and fertile, and that he didn't have oligospermia (low sperm count). I also told him what I learned from fertility expert Dr. Sherman J. Silver: "Avoid hot tubs, saunas, and excessively tight underwear."

According to Dr. Silver, "the person who has been asked to collect semen for analysis will have an abnormally low reading if the first squirt is missed."

Down at the sperm bank, I asked the receptionist if I could go with him "into . . . the room." She said I wasn't allowed in there, so I told RB to come out and signal me when he was done with his blood tests and ready for "the big deposit."

While RB was getting tested for AIDS, hepatitis, and other diseases, I sat in the waiting room reading fertility magazines. (Not quite as exciting as *Poppin' Mamas,* a porno magazine I saw on Forty-second Street for guys who get turned on to pregnant women.)

After a few minutes, I couldn't resist the temptation to see how RB was doing, and when the receptionist walked away, I dashed down the hall and opened up a few doors before I found RB in a small room with a VCR, some porno movies, and a stack of porno magazines on a table. "This place is so sterile, I was having a little trouble," he told me, suddenly looking more enthusiastic. "I came to fluff you up," I told him as I crowded into the room. "Go, boy! Give 'em the first squirt!" I encouraged, doing a Dallas Cowboy Cheerleader thing. Before I could warm up his spermicide, it released a huge specimen. (Most of it reached the cup he was given, but a squirt made a puddle on the cover of *Swank* magazine.) I hid while he opened the door and handed the nurse—who was sitting at a desk in the hallway filing her nails—his full cup of fresh-squeezed "nature's bounty."

Two weeks later, semen analysis confirmed that sperm boy's seed was, indeed, healthy and ready to fertilize the women of America. He could donate up to twice a week, for fifty bucks a load, giving him the chance to improve the human race and turn masturbation into a part-time job.

Continuing our hands-on practicum, our investigations shifted from the reproductive to the recreational. Research boy #5, a twenty-nine-year-old New York City artist, would assist me with my anatomy and physical therapy studies at the local massage parlor.

Calling up places with names like Afternoon Delight and Paradise on the Table, RB asked if they could fax him photos of some of the girls. His scientific inquiries were met with a disconnection to the recorded porno tape, for callers who sounded so undesirable even a massage parlor had to reject them.

I called another place and asked how much it would cost for me to watch. They hung up. The next place, however, was very accommodating and asked if I wanted to participate. The cost: $120 for a half-hour massage plus a $50 voyeur surcharge for me.

At the parlor, an apartment that looked like a doctor's office with a waiting area and three small rooms, we were greeted by Candy, an attractive twenty-two-year-old "relaxation specialist." She had long brown hair and bangs and said her clients included a lot of "tense nine-to-fivers." In a red-brocade-wallpapered room, RB's "leisure consultant" told the now naked research boy to lie on his stomach. She dimmed the lights, put on New Agey music, and rubbed him with oil for five minutes. Then she stripped down to her high heels and thong. As she told RB about her Native American heritage (she looked like a sexy Pocahontas), her beauty raised a half-tepee. When she flipped him on his back, full wigwam was erected. As he felt her butt 'n' boobs, she rubbed his chest, then oiled his tomahawk. Then he asked her to rub his "taint." Soon, it was all over—literally, all over everything, including the table. Included in the price was a free cleanup.

"That last fifteen minutes on my sore muscle was the best part," he said right afterward. Lost in the moment, he was operating on guy time. Little did he know, I timed that part—it lasted only two minutes.

Back at the lab, we analyzed our field data on a scale of one to ten. RB concluded that the hand job rated approximately a 4.5. "It was somewhat mechanical," he reported. "I felt like I had just been milked." He also reported a half hard-on as he left, attributing this to lack of body contact.

"But the fact that I had a naked chick rubbing my research

tool brought the total experience up to a seven point five," he concluded.

After three months of testing, the love lab became crowded with fifty-gallon drums of lubricant, Kleenex boxes that were stacked to the ceiling, and a VCR burnt out from a constant flow of pornos. Also piling up were work-related injuries. On-the-job accidents included one case of rug burn, two scrotal tears, three groin pulls, a yeast infection, four cases of blue balls, and a bruised prostate. Sacrifices made in the name of science. One guy valiantly came into work despite the fact that he had a throbbing hemorrhoid.

Meanwhile, the Chicago branch was diligently at work studying the psychological aspects of autofellatio. After I sent him instructions entitled "Sucking Yourself Off," courtesy of my London colleague, Dr. Tuppy Owens ("Sit against a wall, swing legs over head, bend neck, adjust position"), he called me, worried that if he mastered the technique he would never leave his house. I promised him that if he could do it, I would fly him to New York. When I picked him up at the airport, he was wearing a neck brace.

SURVEY *says*

Keeping Score

In the spirit of scientific inquiry, I sat on my bed in a pink teddy surrounded by 2,571 sex surveys. By the tenth one, I realized that love and sex are two things that people can't get enough of. I was also reminded that while women want more than just sex, men want sex and more sex.

Fortunately, most people revealed more than they were asked. Of the respondents between eighteen and thirty-four years old, 80 percent were male (20 percent gay), and 20 percent female (2 percent lesbian). Eighty-six percent of the surveyees were single, and a startling 21 percent described themselves as celibate, though not necessarily by choice. When one respondent was asked to identify himself as either "sexually active" or "celibate," he circled the second and penciled in "big time—I masturbate a lot." (There's one for the "Duh" file.)

Feelings about first dates were mixed. Most people (30 percent) thought that the first date is "something to look forward to." Twenty-six percent thought it was nerve-racking, and 21 percent thought it was "exhilarating." Considering my last two dates, I had to agree with the 1 percent who said "humiliating."

After being asked "When you're dating someone, do you ever do any of the following?" the most popular response was "Take them out to dinner" (89 percent), followed by "Call them unexpectedly" (81 percent), and "Cook meals for them" (65 percent). An accommodating female wrote in "Do their laundry," while one cunning male penciled in "Check out their roommate." One guy said, "Tie them up." Another said, "Stalk them."

Both men and women said they can tell when someone wants to have sex (82 percent). When asked "What signs do you look for?" "body language" was the first (84 percent), followed by "what they say" (69 percent), and "eye contact" (62 percent). One woman describing herself as bisexual said, "Drippy poon." One twenty-four-year-old male answered, "When they grab your meat."

Gay and straight men had slightly differing opinions on how many dates it takes before they make a move. Gay men average 2.9 dates while straights moved a little more slowly— 4.4 dates. A quarter of the gay guys said they "usually" have sex on the first date, compared to 5 percent of heteros. (One gay male said, "I enjoy being date raped.") Their methods of persuasion differed as well. Straights feature "lying, pleading, begging, and arguing." If these are the techniques they're using, no wonder they're not getting laid.

When it comes to being sexually "correct," most women appreciate being asked before their clothing is torn off, while only half the men think they should bother popping the question before popping a boner. While half the singles agreed that "sexual correctness is necessary at the beginning of a relationship," others questioned the meaning of the term or indicated that the mere sound of it turned them off. The same held true with the word *feminism*, which only 47 percent said they're "sympathetic" to. Meanwhile, the other 53 percent are totally confused by the word's meaning.

Although most responses seemed honest, one question— "Which characteristics are most important in a partner?"— elicited answers from men that sound plausible in theory but not in practice. The top response (61 percent) was "someone you can talk to," followed by "honesty" (49 percent), and "sense of humor" (38 percent). "Intelligent" and "sensitive" followed, while "sexy," "good in bed," and "has money" scraped the bottom of the list. Although most people do want the top three qualities, I guarantee that if you put five supermodels in front of most guys, the "someone you can talk to" concept goes right out the window.

Love, on the other hand, is a more complicated subject, and most people (65 percent) said they are either confused or cynical about it. When asked which movie offers the truest picture of love, the most popular choices were *When Harry Met Sally* and *Ghost*. Considering these statistics, *Dazed and Confused* should have been added to the list. (A survey of my own life revealed my last big love affair to be a tie between *A Nightmare on Elm Street* and *Frankenweenie*).

Feelings about commitment and marriage were similarly mixed. Most married people (61 percent) described marriage as "the ultimate expression of love," while most single people (62 percent) said it's "something I'm not ready for yet." People who were divorced or separated were obviously the most skeptical about marriage. The reasons for getting divorced divided the sexes, with many women mentioning physical and emotional abuse, and men checking "not getting along" and "our sex life died." One married guy wrote, "If she turns out to be a he."

Apparently, once the honeymoon is over, people get a little cranky: 41 percent of ex-marrieds have hit their partners, and 61 percent have been hit (twice as high as the rate for singles). One conclusion to be drawn from this is that togetherness gives people more time to get on each other's nerves. Take a happy couple, throw in emotional, financial, and legal binds, and soon enough someone's getting pounded against the trailer.

Although there seem to be more similarities than differences between gay and straight men, one area they disagree on is marriage for same-sex couples. When asked if gay couples should be allowed to legally marry, 97 percent of gays said yes, while 44 percent of straights said no. I bet if you asked the same men who answered no if first cousins should be allowed to marry, they'd say yes.

When it comes to cheating, men were more likely to view it as having a positive effect on their relationships, while women felt it harmed them. One twenty-year-old Californian wrote, "While filling out this survey, my girlfriend read it and found out that I cheated on her! What now?" He signed it, "In Big Trouble, Santa Barbara." He also marked the question "Why did you cheat on your partner?" with "I was drunk or high," described his sex life as "kinky," and said he had "cave people fantasies."

Men and women always seem to disagree on something, so in response to the question "What do you want more of from your partner?" women wanted "more communication," while men wanted "more blow jobs." Although both sexes said they'd appreciate a little more understanding, women said they wanted things like "less selfishness" or "more affection," while men indicated "more sex" and "less inhibition." One twenty-three-year-old slacker put it simply and said he wanted "money and gifts."

On the subject of porn, men and women are once again coming from different planets. Although the survey revealed that most men (93 percent) and about half the women regularly "self-stimulate," it revealed that men prefer "reading" skin mags (77 percent), renting videos (73 percent), and drooling at topless bars (30 percent). More women prefer to read erotica than men. As someone who read Anaïs Nin at age thirteen, I think the reasons for this are as follows: Most porn videos are aimed at male fantasies, and only the gay ones feature cute guys; there is only one skin mag for straight women that is subscribable to; and there are few strip bars for female enjoyment—unless we go for Chippendales entertainment, which features bad Las Vegas–style movements and embarrassing haircuts. Men also prefer to use their porn alone, while women prefer it with a partner. This is because after watching a porn video by themselves, most women feel like losers, whereas men feel relieved. Personally, I see nothing wrong with having sex by myself; at least my hand doesn't fall asleep or leave right after the big O.

The survey also shows that over a quarter of the respondents don't reveal their sexual secrets or desires to their partners. Yet those same people have no problem telling them to me. Of the eighty-nine questions, the one about sexual fantasies got the most enthusiastic response. The most common sexual fantasy among men was having a three-way (60 percent). The percentage of those who've actually tried it, however, was lower (25 percent). Men said the reason for this fantasy's not becoming reality was that their girlfriends wouldn't let them do it. Women complained that they didn't get enough attention, commitment, or sexual satisfaction as it is, so the last thing they wanted to do was share their crumbs with somebody else. The second favorite sexual fantasy was sex in public places, and the third was group sex. Again, the percentage of those who had tried group sex (13 percent) was lower than those who fantasized about it (38 percent). Let's face it, it's hard enough to get five people to go bowling, let alone organize an orgy.

A number of surveyees said they have tried kinky fun. Over a quarter have indulged in spanking, dominance and submission, and bondage, with others exploring leather, voyeurism, and "sex with best friend's partner." One guy said he likes B&D with light SM because "it's romantic."

"What sexual fantasies do you keep from your partner?" prompted a bunch of write-ins. One twenty-one-year-old said, "I want to put an apple on my penis and have someone beat it off." (It makes creamy applesauce.) One gay man said, "forced sex with straight guys." Many men and women of all persuasions said, "anal sex." Mr. Discreet said, "I want to videotape sex with my girlfriend, then show it to my friends." Another connoisseur of fine entertainment wrote, "watching my girlfriend vogue while she masturbates with a dildo." One beasty boy said, "sex with animals." (*Honey, go get Spot!*)

The question "What's the best sex you've ever had?" also stimulated many true confessions. One neighborly twenty-one-year-old hetero wrote, "doing my forty-year-old neighbor up the ass in the garage." A real family man said, "a three-way with a girl and her sister," adding, "it was exciting because they had a lot of secrets to show me." While men typically focus on location and specific action ("in a self-service car wash—I broke the seat when she came"), women responded to the mood or the entire scenario ("We sat in the backyard on a beautiful Labor Day. I had seven orgasms. We went to the movies afterward").

Definitions of "best sex" tended to involve the possibility of getting caught or doing something unheard of ("making love to a policeman to get out of a ticket") or forbidden ("with a marine on the military base—the uniform was a real turn-on"). Others thought that the best sex involved some form of degradation or loss of control ("she got on all fours and talked filthy"; "she wanted it in every orifice of her body"). One guy recalled, "The first time I had sex with a virgin, I came and she cried." I hate to be the one to break it to him, but those were not tears of joy.

The reasons sex was so great included "she swallowed";

"we got really deep on acid"; "my parents were in the next room"; or "she had great vaginal control." Interestingly, some women felt obligated to apologize for what they liked: "It was so good because it was with a guy with a huge penis. I know it's terrible, but it's true." Men, however, made no apologies: "She had a nice body, but other than that, she was awful," and "Because it was a one-nighter and she barely spoke English."

The survey managed to attract a few extreme cases, from several over twenty-five-year-old virgins to the guy who included "sex with vegetables" and "necrophilia" in his fantasy list. Another came from a thirty-three-year-old male who described his sexuality as "perverted" and said his first requirement in a partner is that she be "good in bed." Although he claims to be "heterosexual," he has had "anal sex with a same-sex partner." He lives with his girlfriend, says he "always gets jealous," but has cheated on her several times and plans on doing it again. He also enjoys "rough sex" and "rape." When asked what he does to woo the women he dates, he said, "Make obscene phone calls."

In response to the question "Who is the sexiest woman alive?" Pamela Anderson and Cindy Crawford topped the list. These two babes were followed by Kim Basinger, Sharon Stone, Madonna, Uma Thurman, Drew Barrymore, Sherilyn Fenn, Janet Jackson, Claudia Schiffer, and several *Sports Illustrated* swimsuit models. One and a half votes trickled in for Anka. I was nominated to join a three-way with Demi Moore by a guy who listed "handcuffs, being dominated, and shaved pussy" among his fantasies. My other vote came from some guy who chose Meat Loaf as the "sexiest man alive."

Women liked Brad Pitt, Antonio Banderas, Mel Gibson, the Baldwin brothers, Henry Rollins, Evan Dando, JFK Jr., Greg Kinnear, and "the guys on *Melrose Place*." Several men voted for themselves. One, who apparently believes in sightings, said Elvis. Gay men picked Tom Cruise and Jean Claude van Damme. Gayboys also chose Madonna as the sexiest woman, followed by Cindy and Julia Roberts. A few people who voted for RuPaul didn't know whether to list her as sexiest man or woman. Some guy voted for himself "in drag."

Many people seemed dissatisfied with some aspect of their relationship. Those who said they were happy with their love lives were unhappy with their sex lives, afraid they might be missing something. They wanted more everything—more sex, more adventurous sex, more affection from their partners, and more partners. Many people said they were looking for something better than what they had. (A quarter of those in relationships say they "plan to break up soon.") Comments ranged from "every relationship has been a disaster" to "my standards are so high I'll never find anyone" to "I have really low standards and still can't find anyone." Despite the discontent, they maintained their optimism, which should provide a glimmer of hope for the future. One hopeful twenty-four-year-old said it best when he answered the question "What's the best sex you've ever had?" with "I don't think I've had it yet."

On-the-**ROAD**

Mark Abrahams

teſting

BABE iN toyLaNd

I'm Playing with
My Sex Toys

When I'm having sex for one, I like to make my "adult entertainment" as playful as possible. But if I'm going to do the job myself, I should have the proper tools. Historically, sex devices have been used since the 1800s when doctors prescribed vibrators to cure "female hysteria." Unlike the "relaxing facial massagers" of the past, the latest vibrators bulge with realistic veins and scrotums and sport names like The Champ, Don Juan, and The Club.

To see what I've been missing, I shopped for my first battery-operated boyfriend. Unfortunately, I wasn't allowed to try things on for size, making it more difficult to decide between the Long Dong Silver with a suction attachment at its base (which the saleswoman at Good Vibrations pointed out works best when it's affixed to a washing machine), the enormous nine-inch Jeff Stryker, or the vibrator with a fore-skin (which looked like it was wearing saggy panty hose.)

Since I was in San Francisco, I felt free to publicly feel up the fleshlike silicone dildos—very humanoid, including a futuristic black rubber dildo that looked as if it belonged to Darth Vader. I also touched one called Shorty. He wasn't long, but he was a fatty. As I picked up the "pocket pal," a small vibrator that fits in a purse, the saleswoman informed me that buying it would be like buying a Yugo. Instead, she recommended the Hitachi Magic Wand, which she consid-ered "the Cadillac of vibrators," which had a huge vibrating head and a high/low switch. I bought one, brought it home, and plugged it in for a pulsating road trip. I tried to lie back and enjoy myself, but the distracting motorized sound it made was about as sensuous as starting up an eggbeater between my legs. When I turned it up to high, it sounded like a ten-speed blender. Afterward, my labia buzzed for an hour on their own.

One trend I noticed while buying toys for us was the pro-liferation of devices for "anal eroticism." I saw plugs and fists so gigantic that using them might require a sphincter trans-plant. As I watched two gay women buy a leather harness with a dildo, the saleswoman told me that many heterosexual women are buying them to "anally penetrate their male part-ners." One called the "vibrating lunar probe" featured "sensu-ous ripples that take you to the moon."

Ready for more fun, I picked up a couple of new boy toys. My first inflatable stud looked like a young Sam Donaldson with a plastic head of dreamy, toupeelike black hair. But I really went for my other blow-up beau, Big John Doll, who was advertised as "a handsome boy, well endowed, in a constantly erect state, 8½ throbbing inches waiting to satisfy your every need." When I got John home, I unfolded him. He looked like a blond Elvis who had been skinned. I blew him up and attached his plastic manhood. I dimmed the lights, got into bed, and ran my fingers through his painted-on chest hair. He was a doll. He felt like a pool raft and smelled like a cross between a new shower curtain and a fresh Barbie. Then I put my arms around him. I turned him on. He hummed. He let me get on top. I rode his firm, rippling plastic. Unselfishly, he was more into giving than receiving. Afterward, I kissed him good-night and tucked him into his box. He didn't say much, but he was an improvement over my last bed partner, whose romantic pillow talk consisted of "Kiss it" and "Sorry I exploded in thirty seconds."

Having satisfied my solo urges, I was ready to watch a guy humiliate himself with a "marital aid." Next stop, Forty-second Street, where I bought a gift for Peter, my new research boy. The Oro-Simulator, "crafted to create the sensation of a lover's mouth," works by sticking the male member into a vinyl sleeve that gets tighter, then looser, when you pump on the squeeze bulb. As my boy got the contraption moving, he looked at me and said, "When I'm through using this thing, do you want it back?" Minutes later, Peter concluded that he would have been better off with his hand. "That was the suckiest suck job I've ever had!" he reported. We agreed that bad sex is one thing, but bad sex with yourself that you paid $69.99 for really makes you feel like a big loser.

Next, it was time for a threesome with Mistress the Talking Vagina. The "other woman" was a plastic glovelike contraption that looked like a pink oven mitt with a control panel that gives a "stimulating vibro performance and tells what she wants and how she wants it."

"I'm slipping my thing into it," Peter reported as he flipped the switch. Then Mistress, who sounded like an English secretary on speakerphone, groaned with heated pants of "Oh, baby," "Deeper, harder, faster," and "It feels so good." "At least she's enthusiastic," he noted. And not at all uptight, we agreed. After Peter spent a few minutes pumping the fake chatty twat, Mistress's "computer-assisted microtechnology" became relentlessly repetitive, and her three broken-record lines gave him a microsofty.

"It feels like I'm having intercourse with a vibrating rubber hot dog bun!" he exclaimed. This was disappointing, especially since a laptop girlfriend seems so convenient for a guy on the go. In the end, though, it was comforting to realize that there is still one job that will never be replaced by a machine.

rock babeſ iN
BOYLAND

Hard-core Grrrl Talk

I'm standing in front of the stage at CBGB's, watching the
lead singer of a punk band stroke his guitar and sing about
how someone he loved dumped him. By the time he gets to
the second song, I am having sexual fantasies about him stage-
diving between my legs.

Even as an eight-year-old, I liked rock-'n'-roll boys. Every
Saturday, I was mysteriously drawn to the neighbor's garage
across the street where I sat cross-legged on the driveway, mes-
merized by five cute older boys who played in a band. Eventually, I would be joined by three or four other girls who sat on
the hot driveway in suburbia, rockin' to the sounds of five
fourteen-year-olds with bad hair. By age eleven and a half, I
had graduated into reading *Tiger Beat* and *Teen Beat,* entering
win-a-date contests with English rock stars. At this age, I

already knew why I liked rock boys; they were rebellious, they were expressive, and they wore tight pants.

As an adult, I continued to like boys in bands, but quickly learned that they make the worst boyfriends. Since then, I've dated mostly artists and actors, but that's another story.

This story begins at Brownies, an East Village bar. I'm watching Fluffer, a local band with five chicks in short skirts and red lips playing music someone describes as "Joni Mitchell on crystal meth." (A fluffer is a stagehand on the set of a porno movie who "fluffs" up the male actors so they don't go limp.) After their last song ("Cocksuck Jamboree") I go to Stingy LuLu's and hang out with them for some grrrl talk and the rock-chick perspective.

As we sit down, a sweating male groupie shows up and hands them a fan letter. Since he is such a dork, there is a collective roll of the eyes as Tanya, the drummer, shows us the letter from Brian, their "humble servant." For their amusement, Brian has drawn a picture of Hitler with his pants down, cutting the cheese. They explain that most of their fans aren't this deranged and usually just want to have sex with all five of them at once. Their admirers, who are seventeen to twenty-two, are unfortunately, they say, "average to below average looking," so they're not into it to get laid, as they accuse some of their male counterparts of doing. As we sit outside on St. Mark's Place, Kathy, the bass player, points out a guy carrying a guitar. "The heroin look is very stylish these days," she says. "Underwashed, undernourished, zits, no underwear, bad breath."

Then we compare notes on what qualities our dream rock guy would possess. We unanimously agree, "Must have brains, must be funny." "If they're not funny, they're history," says Tanya, the drummer. "And talent wouldn't hurt," adds Vanessa, the lead singer. "Maybe a trust fund, you know, something to fall back on," adds Kathy. Other requirements included "big penis," "being good orally," and "toilet cleaner."

Once the basics were covered, we moved into the "premenstrual" segment of our discussion. "The only thing a guy in a band cares about is his hair and his instrument," notes Vanessa. Kathy, who has a degree in forensic psychology, points out that "the guys with the smallest dicks buy the biggest amps."

Then we swap stories of unrequited orgasms. The mere mention of prematurity brought back fond memories for all of us. I shared my story of an Elvis wannabe I dated who looked like Elvis, dressed like Elvis, and was obsessed with watching documentaries on Elvis. The first time I had sex with him, he led me up to his bunk bed with pictures of Elvis hanging above, lighting candles along the way for the "dumpy apartment with candles" bedroom effect. As he took off my shirt and dry-humped me, he rubbed himself against my stomach, the whole time looking up at the King. He didn't have sex *with* me, he had sex *on* me. In fact, he had sex with my stomach.

To add insult to injury, my naval piercing got infected. He was about as satisfying in bed as the drugged-out, passed-out, white-bell-bottomed Elvis.

Then Vanessa told us how she had sex with a drummer on the couch. "He was in between my legs, but he was fucking a slit in the cushion," she told us. "He was fucking the couch."

After we all ate cherry pie, I helped them carry their amps

and instruments home. As we walked through the East Village, a male passersby saw this as an opportunity to catcall. "Hey, baby, can you really play those things?" asked one ignoramus. "Sit on my drum!" screamed another. This is when I decide to write a new song for Fluffer titled "Get a Life and Don't Get Back to Me."

After hanging out with Fluffer, I visited one of the original foxcore girl bands, Babes in Toyland, who live in Chicago. When I meet them at the Rainblo, a low-tech bar with a bombed-out facade in Wicker Park, they are already polluted. Kat, the lead singer, greets me with a kiss on the cheek and a piggyback ride around the bar. We head to the Empty Bottle, where the Babes got their start. When a solo performer onstage starts playing the guitar and singing, "Guys just want to get laid, guys just want to get laid," Kat screams, "Asshole!"

The next day, I watch the Babes rehearse. Their thrashing sound and screeching lyrics ("You know who you are, you dead-meat motherfucker!") are not exactly baby-doll. They have nothing to do with how girls are supposed to act and they like it that way. "Men have this horny look on their faces when we first come onstage, and another when we play," says Kat, squeezing out a bunch of serial burps. "They get intimidated by us, we're too strong for some guys," concurs Maureen, the bass player. "Men want girls who let them walk all over them," she adds before they belt out a song called "Swamp Pussy." Like Hole, they say their most devoted fan demographic is teenage girls. "We also get a lot of lesbians," says Lori, whom they especially go for. "One night a mob of fifteen of them wanted to take me out for a drink," she reports. In contrast, some of their male fans show no respect, heckling them onstage. "Guys yell, 'Take it off!'" says Kat, spitting a huge loogie on the floor. "I tell them, 'Give me a knife and I'll do it for you!'" At Lollapalooza, a bunch of guys yelled, "Show me your tits!" adds Lori. Hearing this, we all decided the crowd would go mental if the next time she yells back, "Shuddup or I'll fuck you up the ass!"

As far as groupies are concerned, the band does not consider itself a "groupie band," but does admit that being in a band "emits a scent." "It changes the power play," says Lori.

They agree that the best fringe benefit of fame is meeting other famous people. Kat makes Lori admit she had sex with Dave Grohl when he was in Nirvana under the stage while Iggy Pop performed. "It was good," she reported, "the kind of sex you get bruises from."

After my girl-band bonding, I realized I had to start my own band: Anka & the Implants. We will wear baby-doll nighties and play hard-core alternative striptease rock with postpunk Emersonian utopian lyrics. ("Eat me, seek me, lick my feet / Bring me to a place where the women aren't dung and the men are well hung . . .")

j o i N   t H e
(S E X)   c L u b

I ' l l   T a k e   M a n h a t t a n

Joining the rest of the horny perverts in New York, I went on a search for sex in the naked city. It was time for another road trip. A quickie to sex establishments. A walking tour of the underbelly of New York. In New York you can get anything you want. For a price, that is. I was looking for cheap thrills and I was willing to pay for them.

"Meet me on Forty-second Street, at Peepland," I said to a guy I had just started dating. "We'll do lunch." As we walked into the place and scrunched into one of the metal sani-pot-like "fantasy booths" arranged in a circle, my lunch date and I put in two tokens ($4), waited for the window to go up, and saw two naked teenage girls who looked as if they had been recruited from the Port Authority bus station standing around smoking cigarettes. This was *not* a Madonna video. As soon as we got there, we had to leave because of the smell: a cross between Mr. Clean and fresh-squeezed spermatozoan. The place was so busy that they had two mopper-uppers.

That night, I took my lunch date, Bill, to the Paradise Club. After paying $15 admission, we were offered a tour of the club, with an "erotic slow-touch dance" for Bill ($20). I had an orange juice ($10). We saw the "lesbian room" where they sell two-girl shows ($50) and went upstairs to a hallway of five-foot-square rooms. Here our "tour guide" told Bill she would take her clothes off and let him touch her breasts ($50). For "more" money, she would give him a "massage." After his dance, Bill told me, "I felt like an idiot paying twenty dollars to grind my meat against her leg." Out on the street, Bill noticed he had been pickpocketed for another $50. You know you're in a classy place when you have to say, "Excuse me while I take off my shoe and get my money out."

Next, Bill and I went to Flash Dancers, a strip joint advertised in the *New York Post*'s sports pages, next to ads for guns and penis enlargements. As waitresses in French-maid outfits pushed drinks ($5), Wendy Whoppers, "international film star," bounced her rock-hard implants around onstage. I told Bill not to get too close in case she swung around and knocked him out.

Instead, Bill got a three-minute table dance ($10)—a teasing, slow grind, removal of top, and heavy eye contact. "They use the same look you get right before you're ready to stick it in," he enthusiastically reported.

Eye contact was followed by butt-to-lap contact for ten seconds. One nerdy guy was so hypnotized that he was unaware of the wet spot forming on the front of his pants. In fact, I've never seen so many wet spots in my life. If the club really wanted to make money, they should rent blow-dryers.

The next night, my friend Cheryl and I headed down to the meatpacking district for some kinky action at the Vault, an S&M club that looks like a cross between a basement and a dungeon. After we each paid $10 (men have to pay $35), we were frisked, reminding us we were here for fun. As we walked in, we felt heavily cruised by dozens of wimpy submissives dying to be dominated. "Count the worms," Cheryl noted.

Everyone was superfriendly. Too friendly. After about five minutes Cheryl and I noticed that we had suddenly attracted a swarm of unattractive, out-of-shape, seminaked masturbators, a scary-looking circle jerk who had surrounded us like the zombies in *Night of the Living Dead*. Something poked me in the back and it wasn't a finger.

Upstairs, the sound of spanking filled the air. "So, where are you girls from?" a couple of guys asked us. *Smack!* "Manhattan." "And where are you from?" we asked. *Boom!* "New Jersey," they said. "We ended up at this place because we saw it on *Jerry Springer.*" *Whack!* Several women were sprawled out on the couches with their skirts pulled down as their boyfriends spanked them with bare hands or paddles. One couple of voyeurs watched through a slit in a Japanese screen as a man with a woman's legs wrapped around his neck spanked her shaved monkey. (According to the Vault's schedule, it was Bald Beaver night.)

Later, a skinny submissive asked if he could lick my boots. "Go ahead, go for it," I told him as he drooled on my patent leather. "And while you're at it, lick my ingrowns." Then we saw him worship another woman's foot for two and a half hours straight without coming up for air. As we watched him going down on her foot, we saw him soften up a bunion and suck off a couple of corns.

As we left the club, we picked up a brochure explaining that "fisting and rimming are not allowed." The only thing left, then, is public masturbation, endless toe sucking, and shaved cooter spanking.

After my free shoe shine, I was ready for some more adult entertainment for women. At the Country Club, Manhattan's *only* strip club for women, my friend Traci and I caught the stirring two-hour Chippendales-like "Man Alive" show. They take a different approach to merchandising the flesh by adding the idea of romance. One beefcake was introduced as "*Playgirl*'s Man of the Decade" and lip-synched to Jon Secada, serenading three women in the audience before ripping off his shirt, stripping to his G-string, and grabbing his crotch.

Then other muscular Adonises did karate movements, humped pillows, struck sexy poses on tops of motorcycles, and whipped towels off their buff, bare butts of steel, as the all-female audience screamed as if they were at a Beatles concert in 1967. These were some rowdy chicks. Every time a guy would bend over, grab his package, or carry a woman from the audience onto the stage and stuff his crotch in her face, the crowd went wild. After the stage show, the strippers jumped into the audience for tips. Like everyone else, Traci and I waved dollar bills as guys came dancing toward us for a hug. The women goosed and grabbed like a bunch of sex-starved,

crazed nymphos. Two of the guys were so cute I paid them $5
each for a kiss. I felt like an idiot paying someone to kiss me.
By the end of the night, Traci and I had each spent $68 ($35
for admission, $10 for two Polaroids, $10 for two kisses, and
$13 for assorted ass grabs). But I did get a "free" poster.

Now that strip joints have become so "respectable" that
businessmen actually take their clients to lunch there, I want to
start taking women to see a show like "Man Alive" for lunch,
where they can eye the fruit salads while bare-butted guys do
table dances. I'm waiting for the day when I can have power
lunches at the equivalent of Hooters. At Wieners, the girls and
I will order hot dogs and hard buns. And beers with big heads
on them.

Jim Radakovich

An Interview
with Mom and Dad

What do you think about sex?

Mom: Sex is very powerful. It drives young men half-crazy. I'm always amused how men light up when a sexy woman walks into the room.

Dad: Sex is a driving force, it motivates male behavior. When men are in their twenties, they're obsessed by it. Yet no matter how old they are, they never stop thinking about it.

I read that after fifty, male testosterone levels start to drop.

Dad: Everybody's but mine.

Who turns you on?

Mom: I like Alex Trebek from *Jeopardy!* He's cute.

And David Chokachi, the new guy from *Baywatch*. I practically have an orgasm every time I see him.

Me, too, I have a multiple. How about you Dad?

Dad: He doesn't do a thing for me.

What was I like when I was little?

Mom: You were very entertaining.

How about when I went through puberty?

Mom: By the time you were eleven and a half we had to get you a bra. By the time you were twelve you were fully developed.

Dad: That's when guys started showing up at the house.

By thirteen I had decided I should start dating.

Dad: I hadn't. I remember the twenty-six-year-old guy who came over to pick you up. I wasn't going to let you out of the house.

I still remember the look on his face when you told him I was still in junior high.

Dad: By the time you were sixteen you were wild.

Mom: I couldn't stop you.

How come you never spanked Jim or me?

Dad: I didn't believe in spanking. Studies now show that spanking encourages violent behavior in children.

But you two are adults. Ever spank each other? You and Mom ought to try it. It's really fun.

Mom: After I read your piece about those dominatrices, I tried to tie Dad up, but he wouldn't let me.

That's because Dad is a dominant, not a submissive.

Mom: What do they call that, a top?

Yeah, Dad's a top. Tops don't like to be tied up. When you first met, what did you notice about each other?

Mom: His personality.

Dad: Her big boobs.

Are you disappointed that I'm not married?

Dad: I'd rather see you single than be married to a loser.

Mom, did you ever regret giving up your opera singing career to have kids?

Mom: I would have felt gypped if I hadn't had children.

Maybe that was a big mistake. Look what you ended up with: "Hello, Mrs. Smith, have you met my daughter? She lives in New York and writes about orgasms, orgies, nudist colonies, and foot fetishes." What kind of guy would you like to see me with?

Dad: You need a real man. Someone with emotional maturity, someone who would treat you with respect.

That would be a switch.

Dad: Women are looking for the same qualities in a man that a father wants for his daughter; someone who will be nice to you and care about you. Someone with intelligence and integrity.

Mom: Someone with a job. You can't do any worse than some of the guys you've gone out with.

What did you think of the story I did where I dressed up like a man for two days?

Dad: It was hard looking at that photo. I looked at it and said, "What happened to my baby girl? My baby doll."

What are your feelings about plastic surgery?

Mom: I'm going in for a face-lift.

Dad: I'm going in for a penis reduction.

What do you think of Pat Buchanan?

Dad: He represents sexual repression. He's too extreme. He's antiabortion, antigay; he's against funding art that has any sexual content . . . He's against more things than he is for. He represents values from one hundred years ago.

Do people say stupid stuff to you about what I do for a living?

Mom: One woman came up to me and whispered, "Is your daughter still writing those dirty articles?" She was so embarrassed she had to whisper. I said, "They're not dirty, they're funny. Why are you so uptight about sex? What's the big deal? Everybody does it. It's part of life." Another woman walked up to me and said she likes you, but doesn't like your subject matter.

Dad: Those two women were projecting the shame they feel about sex on you.

Exactly. What they both need is a good sweaty climax.

Mom: For the first time in their lives.

What was the local reaction here in Maryland when my book came out?

Dad: After a story appeared in the local newspaper, a woman wrote in complaining about the "sinning sex columnist."

She did not feel that you were the right person, as she put it, to "boost the image" of the town. (*Reads from the newspaper*) "Teenagers need another influence with which to scramble their brains. Nice going." What kind of person would write such a letter? So I thought I'd call her up and give her a hard time.

You called her up?

Dad: It turned out she was a born-again Christian. She told me that you and I were going to hell. She told me she objected to the subtitle of your book, *Tales from Below the Belt,* which by the way, she did not read. She objected to the fact that the book review ran in the Sunday paper, which she called "the Lord's Day." Then she told me she would pray for me. To the hypocritical right, sex is sinful except when they are having their nine kids.

Dad, what do you like about what I write?

Dad: You have a unique opportunity to speak for women. Like the feminist writers in the sixties—such as Gloria Steinem—you reveal intimate things that people can identify with.

Right on, Dad, women's libber lover.

Dad: I have great respect for the women's movement. They were courageous. I read Betty Friedan's *The Feminine*

Mystique in 1962, and it had a big influence on me.

What do you dislike most about my job?

Mom: That it puts you in vulnerable situations. I worry about your personal safety.

I have unique occupational hazards. I almost got dragged into the bushes by a sex-starved naked guy at the nudist colony.

Mom: And because you write about sex, men who never met you think they can walk up to you and say anything.

Like, "Can I come on your face?"

Mom: What happened to manners? They don't realize that you are sensitive and romantic. They think you will think they are hilarious for saying that.

Dad: That is really dumb-ass. That's no way to charm a woman. American men need to teach their sons how to be gentlemen; how to seduce, rather than coerce.

I hate when men try to talk me into having sex.

Mom: Begging is a turnoff.

Dad: A man should try to make a woman feel so good that she wants to have sex with him. Because men are so caught up in their own desire, they aren't thinking about what the woman wants. I was so smooth with

Mom that she didn't know what hit her until after it was all over.

That sounds more like a car accident than it does sex.
Do you and Mom still have sex?

Dad: Of course! But now it takes me all night to do once what I once did all night.